Super Simple Spells

270+ Easy Spells

by Witchcraft Magick

Spells

Spells for Money

Love Spells

Spells for Attracting Love

Protection Spells

Beauty Spells

Spells to Recall a Past Life

Healing Spells

Work and Career Spells

Spells for a New Job

Success Spells

Health Spells

Spells for Peace and Harmony

Communication Spells

Spells with Crystals

Good Luck Spells

Binding and Banishing Spells

Clarity Spells

Good Fortune Spells

Blessing and Purification Spells

New Moon Spells

Waxing Moon Spells

Full Moon Spells

Waning Moon Spells

Spell Jar Recipes

Spells for Money

Money spells are a type of magic that are focused on attracting financial prosperity and abundance. These spells can be used to manifest a specific amount of money, attract a new job or career opportunity, or increase the flow of money in your life. Money spells can be performed with candles, crystals, herbs, or other symbolic items and can range from simple affirmations to complex rituals. It is important to remember that while these spells can provide a boost of positive energy and intention towards financial success, they should not be relied on as the sole means of achieving financial stability. Instead, it is recommended to combine spell work with other practical steps such as creating a budget, seeking additional education or training, and being proactive in seeking out financial opportunities.

The Wealth Jar Spell

This spell requires a glass jar, coins, green paper, cinnamon sticks, and a green candle. On the green paper, write your name and the amount of money you wish to attract. Fold the paper and place it in the jar, along with the coins and cinnamon sticks. Light the green candle and place it on top of the jar. Focus on your intention for financial abundance and visualize yourself receiving money. Leave the candle to burn out completely, then keep the jar in a safe place as a symbol of your wealth.

The Green Ribbon Spell

This spell requires a green ribbon, a green candle, and a piece of green cloth. Light the green candle and place it on the green cloth. Tie the green ribbon around the candle, focusing on your intention for financial abundance. Visualize yourself receiving money and imagine the green ribbon symbolizing growth and prosperity. Repeat the following chant three times: "Money come to me, in abundance be. This I ask, so mote it be." Leave the candle to burn out completely, and dispose of the green ribbon in a natural place such as a park or beach.

The Penny Spell

This spell requires a penny, a green candle, and a piece of green cloth. Light the green candle and place it on the green cloth. Hold the penny in your hand and focus on your intention for financial abundance. Visualize yourself receiving money and imagine the penny symbolizing wealth and prosperity. Repeat the following chant three times: "Money come to me, in abundance three. This I ask, so mote it be." Leave the candle to burn out completely, and dispose of the penny in a natural place such as a park or beach.

The Lemon Spell

This spell requires a lemon, nine green leaves, and a piece of green ribbon. Cut the lemon in half and place the nine green leaves inside. Tie the two halves of the lemon together with the green ribbon, forming a bundle. Place the bundle in a prominent place in your home, such as on a windowsill or near your front door. This spell is believed to attract money and financial prosperity by symbolizing the growth of wealth.

The Money Spell with a Lodestone

This spell requires a lodestone, a piece of green cloth, and a green candle. Place the lodestone on the green cloth and light the green candle. Hold the lodestone in your hands and focus on your intention for financial abundance. Visualize money flowing towards you like a magnet, and imagine yourself receiving it easily and effortlessly. Repeat this spell daily until you see results.

The Rosemary Spell

This spell requires rosemary, a blue or purple candle, and a piece of blue or purple cloth. Light the blue or purple candle and place it on the blue or purple cloth. Surround the candle with rosemary, focusing on your intention for financial abundance. Visualize yourself receiving money and imagine the rosemary symbolizing growth and expansion. Repeat the following chant three times: "Money, come to me, in abundance be. Rosemary, bring me growth and prosperity." Allow the candle to burn to its end before putting it out.

The Money Drawing Spell

This spell requires basil leaves, cinnamon, and a green candle. Place the basil leaves and cinnamon in a bowl, and light the green candle. Focus on your intention for financial abundance and visualize yourself receiving money. Repeat the following chant three times: "Money come to me, by and by. Three times three, I ask of thee. This I command, so shall it be." Leave the candle to burn out completely, and dispose of the herbs in the bowl.

The Rice Spell

This spell requires a small amount of rice, a green candle, and a piece of green cloth. Light the green candle and place it on the green cloth. Sprinkle the rice around the candle, focusing on your intention for financial abundance. Visualize yourself receiving money, and imagine the rice symbolizing abundance and prosperity. Leave the candle to burn out completely, and dispose of the rice in a natural place such as a park or beach.

The Sage Smudging Spell

This spell requires sage, a green candle, and a piece of green cloth. Light the green candle and place it on the green cloth. Light the sage and use it to smudge the candle, focusing on your intention for financial abundance. Visualize yourself receiving money and imagine the sage smoke symbolizing purification and protection for your finances. Repeat the following chant three times: "Money come to me, in abundance free. Sage smoke, purify and protect for me." Leave the candle to burn out completely.

The Abundance Affirmation Spell

This spell involves using positive affirmations to attract money. Write down a list of affirmations that focus on abundance, wealth, and prosperity. Examples include "I am worthy of financial abundance" or "Money flows to me easily and effortlessly." Repeat these affirmations daily, either out loud or in your head, while visualizing yourself receiving money.

The Honey Spell

This spell requires a jar of honey, a green candle, and a piece of green cloth. Light the green candle and place it on the green cloth. Pour the honey over the candle, focusing on your intention for financial abundance. Visualize yourself receiving money and imagine the honey symbolizing wealth and prosperity. Repeat the following chant three times: "Money sweet as honey, in abundance come to me. This I ask, so mote it be." Leave the candle to burn out completely, and dispose of the honey in a natural place such as a park or beach.

The Cinnamon Stick Spell

This spell requires cinnamon sticks, a green candle, and a piece of green cloth. Light the green candle and place it on the green cloth. Surround the candle with the cinnamon sticks, focusing on your intention for financial abundance. Visualize yourself receiving money and imagine the cinnamon sticks symbolizing prosperity and growth. Repeat the following chant three times: "Money flow to me, in abundance grow. This I ask, so mote it be." Leave the candle to burn out completely, and dispose of the cinnamon sticks in a natural place such as a park or beach.

The Bay Leaf Spell

This spell requires bay leaves, a green candle, and a piece of green cloth. Light the green candle and place it on the green cloth. Surround the candle with bay leaves, focusing on your intention for financial abundance. Visualize yourself receiving money and imagine the bay leaves symbolizing protection and prosperity. Repeat the following chant three times: "Money come to me, in abundance be. Bay leaves, protect and bring prosperity." Leave the candle to burn out completely.

The Mint Spell

This spell requires mint, a green candle, and a piece of green cloth. Light the green candle and place it on the green cloth. Surround the candle with mint, focusing on your intention for financial abundance. Visualize yourself receiving money and imagine the mint symbolizing growth and prosperity. Repeat the following chant three times: "Money grow for me, in abundance flow. Mint, bring me wealth and let it grow." Leave the candle to burn out completely.

The Cinnamon Spell

This spell requires cinnamon sticks, a red or orange candle, and a piece of red or orange cloth. Light the red or orange candle and place it on the red or orange cloth. Surround the candle with cinnamon sticks, focusing on your intention for financial abundance. Visualize yourself receiving money and imagine the cinnamon sticks symbolizing prosperity and success. Repeat the following chant three times: "Money come my way, in abundance stay. Cinnamon, bring me wealth and success each day." Leave the candle to burn out completely.

The Clove Spell

This spell requires cloves, a yellow or gold candle, and a piece of yellow or gold cloth. Light the yellow or gold candle and place it on the yellow or gold cloth. Surround the candle with cloves, focusing on your intention for financial abundance. Visualize yourself receiving money and imagine the cloves symbolizing good fortune and wealth. Repeat the following chant three times: "Money, come to me, good fortune be. Cloves, bring me wealth, so mote it be." Leave the candle to burn out completely.

The Nutmeg Spell

This spell requires nutmeg, a brown or earth-toned candle, and a piece of brown or earth-toned cloth. Light the brown or earth-toned candle and place it on the brown or earth-toned cloth. Surround the candle with nutmeg, focusing on your intention for financial abundance. Visualize yourself receiving money and imagine the nutmeg symbolizing stability and grounding. Repeat the following chant three times: "Money, come to me, and stay with glee. Nutmeg, bring me stability and security." Leave the candle to burn out completely.

The Ginger Spell

This spell requires ginger, a yellow or gold candle, and a piece of yellow or gold cloth. Light the yellow or gold candle and place it on the yellow or gold cloth. Surround the candle with ginger, focusing on your intention for financial abundance. Visualize yourself receiving money and imagine the ginger symbolizing success and prosperity. Repeat the following chant three times: "Money, come my way, in success stay. Ginger, bring me prosperity each and every day." Leave the candle to burn out completely.

The Sage Spell

This spell requires sage, a green candle, and a piece of green cloth. Light the green candle and place it on the green cloth. Surround the candle with sage, focusing on your intention for financial abundance. Visualize yourself receiving money and imagine the sage symbolizing wisdom and guidance. Repeat the following chant three times: "Money, come to me, in abundance be. Sage, bring me wisdom and prosperity." Permit the candle to burn until it has no wax left.

The Basil Spell

This spell requires basil, a green candle, and a piece of green cloth. Light the green candle and place it on the green cloth. Surround the candle with basil, focusing on your intention for financial abundance. Visualize yourself receiving money and imagine the basil symbolizing prosperity and success. Repeat the following chant three times: "Money, come to me, in abundance be. Basil, bring me success and wealth, so mote it be." Leave the candle to burn out completely.

Love Spells

Love spells are a type of ritual or practice that aims to attract and strengthen romantic love and affection. These spells are performed with the intention of manifesting one's desires for love, enhancing existing relationships, or attracting a new romantic partner. Love spells can vary greatly in their form and complexity, but typically involve the use of symbols, affirmations, candles, crystals, and other materials that hold personal significance for the practitioner. It's important to note that love spells should not be used to manipulate or control others, and should be performed with a focus on self-improvement and creating a positive, loving environment for all involved.

The Rose Quartz Spell

This spell requires a piece of rose quartz, a pink candle, and a piece of pink cloth. Light the pink candle and place it on the pink cloth. Hold the piece of rose quartz in your hands and focus on your intention for love and affection. Visualize yourself attracting love into your life and imagine the rose quartz symbolizing love and compassion. Repeat the following chant three times: "Love come to me, in abundance be. Rose quartz, bring me love and set me free." Let the candle burn until it has completely melted away.

The Rose Petal Spell

This spell requires red rose petals, a pink or red piece of cloth, and a piece of paper. On the piece of paper, write the name of the person you want to attract or the qualities you are seeking in a partner. Surround the paper with the red rose petals and place it on the pink or red cloth. Repeat the following chant three times: "Rose petals, bring love to me. Love and happiness, forever be."

The Lavender Spell

This spell requires lavender, a pink candle, and a piece of pink cloth. Light the pink candle and place it on the pink cloth. Surround the candle with lavender, focusing on your intention for love and affection. Visualize yourself attracting love into your life and imagine the lavender symbolizing purity and passion. Repeat the following chant three times: "Love be pure, in passion endure. Lavender, bring me love and make it secure." Leave the candle to burn out completely.

The Cinnamon Spell

This spell requires cinnamon, a red candle, and a piece of red cloth. Light the red candle and place it on the red cloth. Surround the candle with cinnamon, focusing on your intention for love and passion. Visualize yourself attracting love into your life and imagine the cinnamon symbolizing heat and energy. Repeat the following chant three times: "Love be hot, in passion be got. Cinnamon, bring me love and make it hot." Let the flame consume the candle completely before blowing it out.

The Vanilla Spell

This spell requires vanilla extract, a yellow candle, and a piece of yellow cloth. Light the yellow candle and place it on the yellow cloth. Anoint the candle with vanilla extract, focusing on your intention for love and joy. Visualize yourself attracting love into your life and imagine the vanilla symbolizing sweetness and joy. Repeat the following chant three times: "Love be sweet, in joy complete. Vanilla, bring me love and make it sweet." Leave the candle to burn out completely.

The Jasmine Spell

This spell requires jasmine, a white candle, and a piece of white cloth. Light the white candle and place it on the white cloth. Surround the candle with jasmine, focusing on your intention for love and peace. Visualize yourself attracting love into your life and imagine the jasmine symbolizing peace and calm. Repeat the following chant three times: "Love be calm, in peace be balm. Jasmine, bring me love and make it serene." Let the candle burn until it's completely burned out.

The Love Herbs Spell

This spell requires dried herbs associated with love, such as rose petals, lavender, and jasmine. Place the herbs in a sachet and carry it with you at all times. Repeat the following chant three times: "Herbs of love, bring me my love. Love and happiness, forever be."

The Love Charm Spell

This spell requires a piece of red string and a love charm, such as a heart or a cupid. Tie the love charm to one end of the red string and carry it with you at all times. Repeat the following chant three times: "Charm of love, bring me my love. Love and happiness, forever be."

The Love Crystal Spell

This spell requires a rose quartz crystal and a peaceful place to meditate. Hold the rose quartz crystal in your hand and focus on your intention for love. Repeat the following chant three times: "Rose quartz, bring love to me. Love and happiness, forever be."

The Love Spell Jar

This spell requires a glass jar, pink or red glitter, rose petals, and a piece of paper. On the piece of paper, write the name of the person you want to attract or the qualities you are seeking in a partner. Fill the jar with the rose petals and glitter. Repeat the following chant three times: "Jar of love, bring me my love. Love and happiness, forever be."

Spells for Attracting Love

Spell for Love Attraction

You will need: a pink candle, rose petals, and jasmine essential oil. Anoint the pink candle with the jasmine oil and light it. Sprinkle the rose petals around the candle. Focus on your intention for attracting love and repeat the following incantation three times: "Love, come to me now. Bring me the love of my life, so mote it be." Allow the candle to burn down completely.

Spell for Finding Your Soulmate

You will need: a red candle, a picture of yourself, and a piece of paper. Write down your ideal partner's characteristics on the piece of paper. Light the red candle and hold the picture of yourself in one hand and the piece of paper in the other hand. Repeat the following incantation three times: "Soulmate, come to me now. Help me to find the love of my life, so mote it be." Allow the candle to burn down completely.

Spell for Increasing Romance

You will need: a yellow candle, lavender flowers, and rose essential oil. Anoint the yellow candle with the rose oil and light it. Sprinkle the lavender flowers around the candle. Focus on your intention for increasing romance in your current relationship and repeat the following incantation three times: "Romance, come to me now. Bring more passion and excitement to my relationship, so mote it be." Allow the candle to burn down completely.

Spell for Enhancing Love Energy

You will need: a white candle, rose quartz, and cinnamon. Place the rose quartz near the white candle and light it. Sprinkle cinnamon around the candle. Focus on your intention for enhancing love energy and repeat the following incantation three times: "Love energy, come to me now. Help me to attract and maintain loving relationships, so mote it be." Allow the candle to burn down completely.

Spell for Love and Healing

You will need: a green candle, rose petals, and chamomile essential oil. Anoint the green candle with the chamomile oil and light it. Sprinkle the rose petals around the candle. Focus on your intention for healing past hurts and attracting love and repeat the following incantation three times: "Love and healing, come to me now. Help me to release past hurts and attract love into my life, so mote it be." Allow the candle to burn down completely.

Protection Spells

Protection spells are a form of magic that aim to shield individuals or objects from harm and negative energy. These spells are commonly used for personal safety, physical protection, emotional well-being, and protection against psychic attacks. Protection spells come in many forms, from simple affirmations and visualizations, to elaborate rituals involving candles, herbs, and crystals. Whether you are looking to protect yourself, your home, or your loved ones, protection spells can help you feel empowered and secure.

Protection Jar Spell

Fill a jar with protective herbs, such as rosemary, basil, and bay leaves, along with symbols of protection, such as a piece of black tourmaline or a tiny silver pentacle. Seal the jar with a lid and carry it with you or place it in a location where you need protection.

The Clove Protection Spell

This spell requires cloves, a yellow candle, and a piece of yellow cloth. Light the yellow candle and place it on the yellow cloth. Surround the candle with cloves, focusing on your intention for protection. Repeat the following chant three times: "Protection be my light, darkness take flight. Cloves, keep me safe through day and night." Leave the candle to burn out completely.

The Black Tourmaline Protection Spell

This spell requires black tourmaline crystals, a black candle, and a piece of black cloth. Light the black candle and place it on the black cloth. Surround the candle with black tourmaline crystals, focusing on your intention for protection. Repeat the following chant three times: "Protection be my shield, negativity be repelled. Black tourmaline, keep me safe and secure." Let the candle flame consume all the wax before snuffing it out.

Protection Herbal Bath

Fill a bath with warm water and add a handful of protective herbs, such as rosemary, basil, and lavender. Immerse yourself in the bath, focusing on your intention for protection. Visualize a shield of light surrounding you and repelling negative energies.

Protection Chant

Repeat a simple protection chant, such as "Protection be around me, negativity and harm be gone from me." Repeat the chant several times throughout the day, especially when you're feeling vulnerable or afraid.

Protection Symbols

Wear or carry symbols of protection, such as a pentacle, a piece of black tourmaline, or a hamsa hand. Choose symbols that resonate with you and carry them with you wherever you go.

The Rosemary Protection Spell

This spell requires rosemary, a blue candle, and a piece of blue cloth. Light the blue candle and place it on the blue cloth. Surround the candle with rosemary, focusing on your intention for protection. Repeat the following chant three times: "Protection be my guide, negative energy be denied. Rosemary, keep me safe on all sides." Let the candle run its full course and burn until it's finished.

Protection Crystal Grid

Create a crystal grid with stones that are known for their protective properties, such as black tourmaline, amethyst, or hematite. Arrange the stones in a pattern that you find aesthetically pleasing and spend a few moments meditating on your intention for protection.

The Cinnamon Protection Spell

This spell requires cinnamon sticks, a red candle, and a piece of red cloth. Light the red candle and place it on the red cloth. Surround the candle with cinnamon sticks, focusing on your intention for protection. Repeat the following chant three times: "Protection be my guide, harm be pushed aside. Cinnamon sticks, keep me safe and strong." Permit the candle to burn until it reaches its end.

Rose Quartz and Sage Protection Spell

This spell requires rose quartz crystals, sage, a white candle, and a piece of white cloth. Light the white candle and place it on the white cloth. Surround the candle with rose quartz crystals, focusing on your intention for protection. Next, light the sage and waft the smoke around yourself, your home, or any other objects you want to protect. Repeat the following chant three times: "Protection be around me, safety always be found me. Rose quartz, sage, keep me safe and sound." Leave the candle to burn out completely.

Beauty Spells

Beauty spells are rituals aimed at enhancing one's physical appearance, confidence, and overall well-being. These spells are often performed using symbols, affirmations, and natural ingredients that are believed to bring beauty, charm, and grace. Beauty spells are practiced by many people as a way to boost self-confidence, attract positive attention, and enhance their overall energy. These spells can be performed alone or with the help of a practitioner, and can be done as often as needed to maintain their effects. Whether you're looking to enhance your skin, hair, or overall appearance, there's a beauty spell that can help.

Anti-Aging Spell

Light a pink candle and place it in front of a mirror. Close your eyes and visualize yourself looking younger, with smoother skin and fewer wrinkles. Repeat affirmations such as "I am growing younger and more beautiful every day," or "I am worthy of looking and feeling my best at any age." Keep repeating these affirmations until you feel confident and positive about yourself. Blow out the candle, and repeat this spell whenever you need a boost of confidence and self-love.

Youthful Glow Spell

Light a pink or yellow candle and place it in front of a picture of yourself at your happiest. Sit comfortably in front of the picture and focus on your happy memories. As you focus on the memories, visualize yourself being filled with youthful energy and a radiant glow. Repeat affirmations such as "I am filled with youthful energy" or "I have a radiant and youthful glow." Repeat this spell as often as desired to enhance your youthful appearance.

Hair Growth Spell

Take a green candle and carve your name into it. Light the candle and hold a strand of your hair over the flame, visualizing your hair growing long, thick, and healthy. Repeat affirmations such as "My hair is growing stronger and healthier every day," or "I am worthy of having luscious locks." Hold this visualization for as long as you like, then blow out the candle and keep it in a safe place. Repeat this spell regularly to promote hair growth.

Glowing Skin Spell

Light a green candle and place it in front of a picture of yourself. Sit comfortably in front of the picture and focus on your skin. As you focus on your skin, visualize it becoming smoother, clearer, and more radiant. Repeat affirmations such as "My skin is clear and radiant" or "I have glowing and healthy skin." Repeat this spell as often as desired to enhance the appearance of your skin.

Silky Hair Spell

Light a blue candle and place it in front of a picture of yourself with beautiful hair. Sit comfortably in front of the picture and focus on your hair. As you focus on your hair, visualize it becoming silky, smooth, and shiny. Repeat affirmations such as "My hair is silky and shiny" or "I have beautiful and healthy hair." Repeat this spell as often as desired to enhance the appearance of your hair.

Confidence Boost Spell

Light an orange candle and place it in front of a picture of yourself feeling confident. Sit comfortably in front of the picture and focus on your confidence. As you focus on your confidence, visualize it growing stronger and more radiant. Repeat affirmations such as "I am confident and radiant" or "I am beautiful and confident in my own skin." Repeat this spell as often as desired to boost your confidence and enhance your beauty.

Radiant Skin Spell

Light a white candle and place it in front of a mirror. Close your eyes and visualize yourself with glowing, radiant skin. Repeat affirmations such as "I am beautiful, inside and out," or "I deserve to feel confident in my skin." Keep repeating these affirmations until you feel confident and positive about yourself. Blow out the candle, and repeat this spell whenever you need a boost of confidence and self-love.

Radiant Beauty Spell

Light a white candle and place it in front of a mirror. Sit comfortably in front of the mirror and focus on your reflection. As you look at yourself, visualize your inner and outer beauty shining bright like the candle. Repeat affirmations such as "I am beautiful inside and out" or "I radiate beauty and confidence." Repeat this spell as often as desired to enhance your inner and outer beauty.

Nail Growth Spell

Take a yellow candle and carve your name into it. Light the candle and hold your hands over the flame, visualizing your nails growing strong and healthy. Repeat affirmations such as "My nails are growing stronger and healthier every day," or "I am worthy of having beautiful, healthy nails." Hold this visualization for as long as you like, then blow out the candle and keep it in a safe place. Repeat this spell regularly to promote nail growth.

Glowing Complexion Spell

Light a blue candle and place it in front of a mirror. Close your eyes and visualize yourself with a healthy, glowing complexion. Repeat affirmations such as "My skin is radiant and glowing," or "I am worthy of having beautiful, healthy skin." Keep repeating these affirmations until you feel confident and positive about yourself. Blow out the candle, and repeat this spell whenever you need a boost of confidence and self-love.

Spells to Recall a Past Life

Past life recall spells, also known as regression spells, are magical practices aimed at accessing memories and experiences from past lives. These spells are often used as a means of personal growth and healing, as they allow individuals to gain insight into their past experiences and understand how they may be affecting their present lives. Past life recall spells can also be used to help individuals connect with their spiritual guides or higher selves, or to discover hidden talents or gifts. Many different techniques and rituals can be used for past life recall spells, including meditation, visualization, and dream work, and they can be tailored to suit the individual's specific needs and intentions. Whether you're seeking personal insight or a deeper connection with your spiritual self, past life recall spells can be a powerful tool for growth and self-discovery.

Rose Quartz Spell

This spell requires rose quartz crystals, a pink candle, and a piece of pink cloth. Light the pink candle and place it on the pink cloth. Surround the candle with rose quartz crystals, focusing on your intention to recall past lives. Hold a rose quartz crystal in each hand and visualize yourself traveling back in time. Repeat the following chant three times: "Memories of past lives, be revealed to me. Rose quartz, guide me to what is meant to be seen." Leave the candle to burn out completely.

Lavender Spell

This spell requires dried lavender, a purple candle, and a piece of purple cloth. Light the purple candle and place it on the purple cloth. Surround the candle with dried lavender, focusing on your intention to recall past lives. Close your eyes and breathe in the scent of the lavender, imagining yourself in a peaceful, relaxed state. Repeat the following chant three times: "Past lives, come to light. Lavender, bring me insight." Leave the candle to burn out completely.

Sage Spell

This spell requires sage, a white candle, and a piece of white cloth. Light the white candle and place it on the white cloth. Surround the candle with sage, focusing on your intention to recall past lives. Wave the sage around the candle to cleanse the energy and create a peaceful atmosphere. Repeat the following chant three times

"Past lives, be revealed. Sage, help me to heal." Leave the candle to burn out completely.

Amber Spell

This spell requires amber, a yellow candle, and a piece of yellow cloth. Light the yellow candle and place it on the yellow cloth. Surround the candle with amber, focusing on your intention to recall past lives. Hold an amber stone in your hand and visualize a bright light shining on your memories, illuminating them. Repeat the following chant three times: "Memories of past lives, be brought to life. Amber, bring me knowledge and light." Leave the candle to burn out completely.

Amethyst Spell

This spell requires amethyst crystals, a purple candle, and a piece of purple cloth. Light the purple candle and place it on the purple cloth. Surround the candle with amethyst crystals, focusing on your intention to recall past lives. Hold an amethyst crystal in each hand and imagine yourself being surrounded by a protective energy. Repeat the following chant three times: "Past lives, be revealed to me. Amethyst, protect me and set me free." Leave the candle to burn out completely.

Moonstone Spell

This spell requires moonstone crystals, a silver candle, and a piece of silver cloth. Light the silver candle and place it on the silver cloth. Surround the candle with moonstone crystals, focusing on your intention to recall past lives. Hold a moonstone crystal in each hand and visualize the soft, glowing light of the moon illuminating your past. Repeat the following chant three times: "By moon's gentle glow, past lives now show. Moonstone, guide me to what I need to know." Leave the candle to burn out completely.

Healing Spells

Healing spells can be used to promote physical, emotional, or spiritual well-being. These spells can help to alleviate pain, reduce stress and anxiety, and boost the body's natural ability to heal. By using visualization, affirmations, and other techniques, healing spells can help to create positive change and promote overall health and happiness. Whether you're seeking to heal a specific issue or simply wish to maintain a healthy, balanced state of being, healing spells can be an effective tool to support your journey towards wellness.

The Rose Quartz Spell

This spell requires a rose quartz crystal and a quiet place where you won't be disturbed. Hold the rose quartz in your hands and focus on your intention for healing. Visualize yourself surrounded by a soft, pink light, which represents the love and healing energy of the rose quartz. Repeat the following affirmation three times: "I am worthy of love and healing. The energy of this rose quartz crystal surrounds me and brings me peace."

The Lavender Spell

This spell requires dried lavender, a white candle, and a piece of white cloth. Light the white candle and place it on the white cloth. Surround the candle with dried lavender, focusing on your intention for healing. Visualize yourself surrounded by a soothing, blue-purple light, which represents the calming and healing properties of lavender. Repeat the following affirmation three times: "I am calm, I am healed. The lavender soothes me, and I am whole."

The Eucalyptus Spell

This spell requires dried eucalyptus leaves, a green candle, and a piece of green cloth. Light the green candle and place it on the green cloth. Surround the candle with dried eucalyptus leaves, focusing on your intention for healing. Visualize yourself surrounded by a vibrant, green light, which represents the rejuvenating and healing properties of eucalyptus. Repeat the following affirmation three times: "I am renewed, I am healed. The eucalyptus revitalizes me, and I am strong."

The Sage Spell

This spell requires dried sage, a white candle, and a piece of white cloth. Light the white candle and place it on the white cloth. Surround the candle with dried sage, focusing on your intention for healing. Visualize yourself surrounded by a bright, white light, which represents the purifying and healing properties of sage. Repeat the following affirmation three times: "I am pure, I am healed. The sage cleanses me, and I am free."

The Amber Spell

This spell requires amber beads or an amber gemstone, and a quiet place where you won't be disturbed. Hold the amber in your hands and focus on your intention for healing. Visualize yourself surrounded by a warm, golden light, which represents the healing energy of amber. Repeat the following affirmation three times: "I am warm, I am healed. The amber soothes me, and I am strong."

The Healing Water Spell

For this spell, you will need a bowl of clean water, a quiet space, and a comfortable place to lie down. Hold your hands over the bowl of water, focusing on your intention for healing. Visualize a blue light surrounding your body, filling it with positive energy and washing away any negative energy. Repeat the following affirmations three times

"I am healed, I am purified, I am filled with water and life." Dip your hands into the water and allow its coolness to soothe and heal your body.

Healing Candle Spell

Choose a green or pink candle to represent healing and love. Light the candle and place it in a safe place. Sit in front of the candle and visualize yourself being surrounded by light and healing energy. Repeat this visualization for as long as you like, and then extinguish the candle. Repeat this spell as often as needed.

The Healing Herbs Spell

For this spell, you will need a selection of healing herbs (such as lavender, chamomile, or mint), a quiet space, and a comfortable place to lie down. Hold the herbs in your hand, close your eyes, and focus on your intention for healing. Visualize a green light surrounding your body, filling it with positive energy and washing away any negative energy. Repeat the following affirmations three times: "I am healed, I am refreshed, I am filled with life and energy." Place the herbs on your chest and allow yourself to relax and soak in their healing energy.

The Healing Earth Spell

For this spell, you will need a quiet space and a comfortable place to lie down. Lie down on the ground and focus on your intention for healing. Visualize a brown light surrounding your body, filling it with positive energy and washing away any negative energy. Repeat the following affirmations three times: "I am healed, I am grounded, I am filled with earth and strength." Allow the energy of the earth to support and heal your body.

The Healing Sound Spell

For this spell, you will need a singing bowl or other musical instrument, a quiet space, and a comfortable place to lie down. Play the instrument, focusing on your intention for healing. Visualize a golden light surrounding your body, filling it with positive energy and washing away any negative energy. Repeat the following affirmations three times

"I am healed, I am rejuvenated, I am filled with sound and vibration." Allow the sounds to wash over you and soothe your mind and body.

The Healing Crystal Spell

For this spell, you will need a healing crystal of your choice (such as amethyst, rose quartz, or black tourmaline), a quiet space, and a comfortable place to lie down. Hold the crystal in your hand, close your eyes, and focus on your intention for healing. Visualize a white light surrounding your body, filling it with positive energy and washing away any negative energy. Repeat the following affirmations three times

"I am healed, I am whole, I am filled with light and love." Place the crystal on your chest and allow yourself to relax and soak in its healing energy.

Work and Career Spells

If you're looking to enhance your career or find success in your work life, try incorporating magic and spells into your daily routine. Whether you're seeking a promotion, a new job, or simply want to improve your current work environment, these spells can help you achieve your goals and bring positivity and prosperity to your professional life. These spells can help you reach your full potential in the workplace. By focusing your energy and intention on your career aspirations, you can unlock the full potential of your skills and talents, and attract success in all areas of your life.

The Green Aventurine Spell

This spell requires a green aventurine crystal, a green candle, and a piece of green cloth. Light the green candle and place it on the green cloth. Hold the green aventurine crystal in your hand and focus on your intention for career success. Visualize yourself excelling in your field and imagine the green aventurine crystal symbolizing growth and prosperity. Repeat the following chant three times: "Success come to me, in my career be. Green aventurine, bring me growth and prosperity." Leave the candle to burn out completely.

Spell for a Raise

You will need: a red candle, mint, and a piece of paper. Write down your intention for a raise or promotion on the piece of paper. Light the red candle and sprinkle the mint around it. Hold the piece of paper in your hands and focus on your intention. Repeat the following incantation three times: "Raise or promotion, come to me now. Help me to achieve financial success, so mote it be." Allow the candle to burn down completely.

The Clove Spell

This spell requires cloves, a yellow candle, and a piece of yellow cloth. Light the yellow candle and place it on the yellow cloth. Surround the candle with cloves, focusing on your intention for work and career success. Visualize yourself achieving your goals and imagine the cloves symbolizing success and achievement. Repeat the following chant three times: "Work success be mine, in my career shine. Cloves, bring me victory and success." Leave the candle to burn out completely.

The Cinnamon Spell

This spell requires cinnamon sticks, a red candle, and a piece of red cloth. Light the red candle and place it on the red cloth. Surround the candle with cinnamon sticks, focusing on your intention for work and career success. Visualize yourself rising to the top of your field and imagine the cinnamon sticks symbolizing energy and motivation. Repeat the following chant three times: "Career success come, with energy and motion. Cinnamon, bring me power and success." Leave the candle to burn out completely.

The Nutmeg Spell

This spell requires nutmeg, a brown candle, and a piece of brown cloth. Light the brown candle and place it on the brown cloth. Surround the candle with nutmeg, focusing on your intention for work and career success. Visualize yourself reaching new heights in your field and imagine the nutmeg symbolizing abundance and prosperity. Repeat the following chant three times: "Work success arrive, with abundance and thrive. Nutmeg, bring me wealth and success." Leave the candle to burn out completely.

The Star Anise Spell

This spell requires star anise, a purple candle, and a piece of purple cloth. Light the purple candle and place it on the purple cloth. Surround the candle with star anise, focusing on your intention for work and career success. Visualize yourself making a name for yourself in your field and imagine the star anise symbolizing recognition and success. Repeat the following chant three times: "Career success be, with recognition and glee. Star anise, bring me fame and success." Leave the candle to burn out completely.

Spell for Confidence in the Workplace

You will need: a yellow candle, lavender, and a piece of paper. Write down your intention for confidence and success in the workplace on the piece of paper. Light the yellow candle and sprinkle the lavender around it. Hold the piece of paper in your hands and focus on your intention. Repeat the following incantation three times: "Confidence and success, come to me now. Help me to thrive in the workplace, so mote it be." Allow the candle to burn down completely.

Spell for Good Relationships in the Workplace

You will need: a blue candle, rose petals, and a piece of paper. Write down your intention for positive and harmonious relationships with coworkers and superiors on the piece of paper. Light the blue candle and sprinkle the rose petals around it. Hold the piece of paper in your hands and focus on your intention. Repeat the following incantation three times: "Positive relationships, come to me now. Help me to work in harmony with others, so mote it be." Allow the candle to burn down completely.

Spells for a New Job

Finding a new job can be a challenging and stressful experience. However, incorporating magic and spells into your job search can help bring focus, clarity, and positive energy to the process. The following spells can aid in attracting job opportunities, enhancing your interview skills, and increasing your confidence during the job search. Whether you are seeking a new career path or just need a change, these spells can provide support and guidance on your journey towards finding your perfect job. Remember, spell work is most effective when combined with action and persistence in your job search.

New Job Candle Spell

Light a green or gold candle and place it in a safe place. Sit in front of the candle and visualize yourself landing your dream job and being surrounded by abundance and prosperity. Repeat this visualization for as long as you like, and then extinguish the candle. Repeat this spell as often as you need a boost of positive energy for your job search.

Job Search Crystal Spell

Choose a clear quartz crystal, which is known for amplifying energy and intention. Hold the crystal in your hand and focus on your desired job outcome. Visualize yourself successfully landing your dream job, and repeat a positive affirmation such as "I am worthy of my perfect job and I will attract it easily." Place the crystal in your pocket or carry it with you while job searching.

Job Confidence Spell

Light a white candle and place it in a safe place. Sit in front of the candle and visualize yourself radiating confidence and positivity during job interviews. Repeat this visualization for as long as you like, and then extinguish the candle. Repeat this spell before each interview to help boost your confidence and attract positive energy.

Resume Blessing Spell

Write your resume on a piece of paper and bless it with your intention. Hold the paper in both hands and say something like: "May this resume bring me the perfect job opportunity and open doors to my success." Place the blessed resume in a safe place and repeat this spell before sending it out for any job applications.

Job Networking Spell

Choose a yellow or orange candle to represent networking and communication. Light the candle and place it in a safe place. Sit in front of the candle and visualize yourself making valuable connections and networking opportunities that will lead to your dream job. Repeat this visualization for as long as you like, and then extinguish the candle. Repeat this spell before attending any networking events or making connections in your job search.

Spell for a New Career Opportunity

You will need: a green candle, rosemary, and a piece of paper. Write down your intention for finding a new job or career opportunity on the piece of paper. Light the green candle and sprinkle the rosemary around it. Hold the piece of paper in your hands and focus on your intention. Repeat the following incantation three times: "New career opportunities, come to me now. Help me to find the perfect job, so mote it be." Allow the candle to burn down completely.

Spell for a Job Interview

You will need: a white candle, basil, and a piece of paper. Write down your intention for a successful job interview on the piece of paper. Light the white candle and sprinkle the basil around it. Hold the piece of paper in your hands and focus on your intention. Repeat the following incantation three times: "Successful job interview, come to me now. Help me to make a positive impression, so mote it be." Allow the candle to burn down completely.

Success Spells

Success spells are a type of magic that aim to bring success and abundance into various areas of life, such as career, business, education, and personal goals. These spells are believed to tap into the power of positive energy, intention, and manifestation to attract success and remove any obstacles or negative influences that might stand in the way. By performing these spells, practitioners aim to align themselves with their goals and boost their chances of achieving success. Success spells can be simple or complex, and may involve ritual elements such as candles, crystals, herbs, affirmations, visualization, or prayer. Whether you are seeking a promotion at work, starting a new business, or pursuing your dreams, success spells can help you focus your mind and energies towards your desired outcome.

The Cinnamon Spell

This spell requires cinnamon, a yellow candle, and a piece of yellow cloth. Light the yellow candle and place it on the yellow cloth. Sprinkle cinnamon around the candle, focusing on your intention for success in your career or other endeavors. Visualize yourself achieving your goals and imagine the cinnamon symbolizing power and success. Repeat the following chant three times: "Success be mine, let my efforts shine. Cinnamon, bring me power, let success be mine." Leave the candle to burn out completely.

The Clove Spell

This spell requires cloves, a red candle, and a piece of red cloth. Light the red candle and place it on the red cloth. Surround the candle with cloves, focusing on your intention for success in your career or other endeavors. Visualize yourself achieving your goals and imagine the cloves symbolizing protection and success. Repeat the following chant three times: "Success be mine, let my path be fine. Cloves, protect me, let success be mine." Leave the candle to burn out completely.

The Nutmeg Spell

This spell requires nutmeg, a green candle, and a piece of green cloth. Light the green candle and place it on the green cloth. Sprinkle nutmeg around the candle, focusing on your intention for success in your career or other endeavors. Visualize yourself achieving your goals and imagine the nutmeg symbolizing growth and success. Repeat the following chant three times: "Success grow for me, let my efforts show. Nutmeg, bring me growth, let success be mine." Leave the candle to burn out completely.

The Star Anise Spell

This spell requires star anise, a purple candle, and a piece of purple cloth. Light the purple candle and place it on the purple cloth. Surround the candle with star anise, focusing on your intention for success in your career or other endeavors. Visualize yourself achieving your goals and imagine the star anise symbolizing protection and success. Repeat the following chant three times: "Success be mine, let my path be divine. Star anise, protect me, let success be mine." Leave the candle to burn out completely.

The Ginger Spell

This spell requires ginger, a yellow candle, and a piece of yellow cloth. Light the yellow candle and place it on the yellow cloth. Grate ginger over the candle, focusing on your intention for success in your career or other endeavors. Visualize yourself achieving your goals and imagine the ginger symbolizing power and success. Repeat the following chant three times: "Success be mine, let my power shine. Ginger, bring me power, let success be mine." Leave the candle to burn out completely.

Health Spells

Health spells are a type of magic that is used to promote physical and mental well-being. This type of spell can be used to treat specific ailments, increase overall energy and vitality, or protect against illness and injury. Health spells can be performed using a variety of methods, including visualization, affirmations, herbal magic, and candle magic. By tapping into the power of intention and the energy of the universe, practitioners of health spells hope to improve their health and live a more fulfilling life. Whether you are seeking relief from a specific health issue or simply seeking to boost your overall well-being, health spells may be worth considering as a complementary or alternative form of treatment.

Herbal Bath Spell

Fill a bath with warm water and add a handful of dried lavender, rose petals, and chamomile. Light a white candle and place it near the bath. Close your eyes and visualize yourself surrounded by a warm and healing light. Repeat the following affirmation three times: "I am healthy, I am strong, I am whole." Soak in the bath for at least 20 minutes, allowing the herbs to work their magic.

Gratitude Spell

Write down 10 things you are grateful for on a piece of paper. Hold the paper in your hands and close your eyes. Visualize yourself surrounded by a warm and loving light. Repeat the following affirmation three times: "I am grateful for my health, for my strength, for my life." Fold the paper and carry it with you, or bury it in the earth.

Green Light Spell

Close your eyes and visualize yourself surrounded by a bright green light. Imagine this light entering your body and healing every cell, every organ, and every system. Repeat the following affirmation three times: "I am surrounded by a healing green light, I am strong, I am healthy." Keep the visualization in your mind for at least 5 minutes, or longer if you wish.

Food Magic Spell

Choose foods that are nourishing for your body and prepare them with love. Before eating, bless the food by holding your hands over it and saying: "This food brings me health, this food brings me strength, this food brings me healing." Enjoy the food, savoring every bite and feeling its positive energy nourishing your body.

Healing Crystal Spell

Choose a crystal that resonates with you, such as amethyst, rose quartz, or clear quartz. Cleanse the crystal in salt water and place it on a piece of green cloth. Close your eyes and hold the crystal, visualizing yourself surrounded by a warm and healing light. Repeat the following affirmation three times: "This crystal brings me health, this crystal brings me strength, this crystal brings me healing." Keep the crystal with you, or place it in a special place where you can see it often.

Green Aventurine Spell

This spell requires green aventurine stones and a green candle. Light the green candle and hold the green aventurine stones in your hands, focusing on your intention for good health and wellness. Repeat the following chant three times: "Green aventurine, bring me health and vitality. Let my body be strong, let my mind be free." Place the green aventurine stones near the green candle and leave the candle to burn out completely.

Rose Quartz Spell

This spell requires rose quartz stones and a pink candle. Light the pink candle and hold the rose quartz stones in your hands, focusing on your intention for emotional and physical healing. Repeat the following chant three times: "Rose quartz, bring me love and light. Heal my heart, heal my sight." Place the rose quartz stones near the pink candle and leave the candle to burn out completely.

Sage Smudge Stick Spell

This spell requires a sage smudge stick and a feather. Light the sage smudge stick and use the feather to waft the smoke over your body, focusing on your intention for physical and spiritual healing. Repeat the following chant three times: "Sage smoke, cleanse and heal. Remove all negativity, let me feel." Wave the sage smudge stick over your body until the smoke has cleared.

Essential Oil Spell

This spell requires your favorite essential oil and a diffuser. Fill the diffuser with water and add a few drops of your favorite essential oil. Focus on your intention for healing as you inhale the scented steam. Repeat the following chant three times: "Essential oil, heal and soothe. Let my body feel refreshed, let my spirit be renewed." Inhale the scented steam until you feel relaxed and refreshed.

Crystal Grid Spell

This spell requires a variety of healing crystals, such as amethyst, black tourmaline, and clear quartz. Arrange the crystals in a grid pattern, focusing on your intention for physical and emotional healing. Repeat the following chant three times: "Crystals, heal and protect. Let my body be strong, let my mind be correct." Leave the crystal grid in place until you feel a sense of healing and rejuvenation.

Spells for Peace and Harmony

Peace and harmony spells are magical rituals aimed at promoting inner peace and balance, as well as fostering harmonious relationships with others. These spells can help you to dispel negative emotions, reduce stress and anxiety, and cultivate feelings of love, compassion, and empathy. They can also help to attract positive energy and good luck into your life, and provide a sense of stability and security in uncertain times. Whether you are seeking personal growth or seeking to improve your relationships with others, peace and harmony spells can provide a powerful tool for manifesting your desires.

Lavender and Rose Spell

This spell requires dried lavender and rose petals, a glass jar, and a white candle. Fill the jar with the lavender and rose petals, and light the white candle. Focus on your intention for peace and harmony in your life, and imagine a warm, white light spreading peace throughout the jar and into your life. Repeat the following affirmation three times: "Peace and harmony, come to me. Lavender and rose, bring serenity." Leave the candle to burn out completely.

Spell for Inner Peace

You will need: a blue candle, a piece of paper, and lavender. Light the blue candle and sprinkle the lavender around it. Write down your intention for inner peace on the piece of paper. Hold the piece of paper in your hands and focus on your intention. Repeat the following incantation three times: "Inner peace, come to me now. Help me to find serenity within, so mote it be." Allow the candle to burn down completely.

Chamomile Spell for Peace and Harmony

For this spell, you will need chamomile, a glass jar, and a piece of white cloth. Fill the jar with chamomile, making sure to pack it tightly. Tie the piece of white cloth around the neck of the jar and secure it with a knot. As you do this, focus on your intention for peace and harmony to be brought into your life. Hold the jar in your hands and repeat the following chant three times: "Peace and harmony, come to me. Chamomile, make it so, naturally." Place the jar in a quiet place and allow it to work its magic.

Sage Smudging Spell

This spell requires sage, a feather, and a lighter. Light the sage, and use the feather to waft the smoke around your space, focusing on your intention for peace and harmony. Repeat the following affirmation three times: "Sage smoke, bring peace to me. Fill my life with harmony and serenity."

Spell for Peaceful Home

You will need: a white candle, a piece of paper, and sage. Write down your intention for a peaceful home on the piece of paper. Light the white candle and sprinkle the sage around it. Hold the piece of paper in your hands and focus on your intention. Repeat the following incantation three times: "Peaceful home, come to me now. Help me to create a sanctuary of calm and serenity, so mote it be." Allow the candle to burn down completely.

Spell for Harmony in Relationships

You will need: two pink candles, a piece of paper, and rose petals. Write down your intention for harmony in your relationships on the piece of paper. Light the two pink candles and sprinkle the rose petals around them. Hold the piece of paper in your hands and focus on your intention. Repeat the following incantation three times: "Harmony in relationships, come to me now. Help me to find peace and balance in my interactions with others, so mote it be." Allow the candles to burn down completely.

Lavender Spell for Peace and Harmony

For this spell, you will need lavender, a glass jar, and a piece of white cloth. Fill the jar with lavender, making sure to pack it tightly. Tie the piece of white cloth around the neck of the jar and secure it with a knot. As you do this, focus on your intention for peace and harmony to be brought into your life. Hold the jar in your hands and repeat the following chant three times: "Peace and harmony, come to me. Lavender, make it so, naturally." Place the jar in a quiet place and allow it to work its magic.

Spell for Global Peace

You will need: a green candle, a piece of paper, and frankincense. Write down your intention for global peace on the piece of paper. Light the green candle and sprinkle the frankincense around it. Hold the piece of paper in your hands and focus on your intention. Repeat the following incantation three times: "Global peace, come to me now. Help me to bring calm and understanding to the world, so mote it be." Allow the candle to burn down completely.

White Sage Spell for Peace and Harmony

For this spell, you will need white sage, a glass jar, and a piece of white cloth. Fill the jar with white sage, making sure to pack it tightly. Tie the piece of white cloth around the neck of the jar and secure it with a knot. As you do this, focus on your intention for peace and harmony to be brought into your life. Hold the jar in your hands and repeat the following chant three times: "Peace and harmony, come to me. White sage, make it so, naturally." Place the jar in a quiet place and allow it to work its magic.

Ocean Spell

This spell requires a glass jar, water, blue food coloring, and seashells. Fill the jar with water, and add a few drops of blue food coloring to represent the ocean. Place the seashells in the jar, and focus on your intention for peace and harmony. Imagine yourself being surrounded by the peaceful energy of the ocean, and repeat the following affirmation three times: "Ocean waves, bring peace my way. Wash away all stress and disharmony."

Nature Spell

This spell requires you to go outside into nature and find a peaceful spot. Sit down and focus on your intention for peace and harmony. Imagine the peaceful energy of nature washing over you, filling you with peace and calm. Repeat the following affirmation three times: "Nature, bring peace to me. Fill my life with harmony and serenity."

Rose Petal Spell for Peace and Harmony

For this spell, you will need rose petals, a glass jar, and a piece of white cloth. Fill the jar with rose petals, making sure to pack them tightly. Tie the piece of white cloth around the neck of the jar and secure it with a knot. As you do this, focus on your intention for peace and harmony to be brought into your life. Hold the jar in your hands and repeat the following chant three times: "Peace and harmony, come to me. Rose petals, make it so, naturally." Place the jar in a quiet place and allow it to work its magic.

Spell for Harmonious Workplace

You will need: a yellow candle, a piece of paper, and chamomile. Write down your intention for a harmonious workplace on the piece of paper. Light the yellow candle and sprinkle the chamomile around it. Hold the piece of paper in your hands and focus on your intention. Repeat the following incantation three times: "Harmonious workplace, come to me now. Help me to find balance and cooperation in my professional life, so mote it be." Allow the candle to burn down completely.

Incense Spell

This spell requires incense, a lighter, and a quiet place. Light the incense, and focus on your intention for peace and harmony. Imagine the scent of the incense filling your space with peace and calm. Repeat the following affirmation three times: "Incense smoke, bring peace to me. Fill my life with harmony and serenity."

Gratitude Spell

This spell requires a piece of paper and a pen. Write down 10 things you are grateful for, and focus on your intention for peace and harmony. Imagine a warm, golden light spreading peace and gratitude throughout your life. Repeat the following affirmation three times: "Gratitude, bring peace to me. Fill my life with harmony and serenity."

Chanting Spell

This spell requires you to find a quiet place where you can chant comfortably. Focus on your intention for peace and harmony, and repeat the following chant three times: "Om shanti, shanti, shanti. May peace and harmony reign in me."

Moon Spell

This spell requires you to perform it during a full moon. Stand outside and focus on your intention for peace and harmony. Imagine the energy of the full moon washing over you, filling you with peace and calm. Repeat the following affirmation three times: "Full moon, bring peace to me. Fill my life with harmony and serenity."

Rose Quartz Spell for Peace and Harmony

For this spell, you will need rose quartz crystals, a glass jar, and a piece of white cloth. Fill the jar with the rose quartz crystals, making sure to pack them tightly. Tie the piece of white cloth around the neck of the jar and secure it with a knot. As you do this, focus on your intention for peace and harmony to be brought into your life. Hold the jar in your hands and repeat the following chant three times: "Peace and harmony, come to me. Rose quartz, make it so, naturally." Place the jar in a quiet place and allow it to work its magic.

Communication Spells

Communication spells are a form of magic aimed at enhancing and improving the flow of communication between two individuals or within a group. These spells are designed to help individuals effectively express themselves and understand others better. Communication spells can be used in a variety of situations, whether you're seeking to improve your relationships with friends and family, or looking to enhance your professional communication skills. With the right intentions, visualization, and ritual, these spells can help you create positive and meaningful connections with others.

Spell for Conflict Resolution

You will need: a white candle, rose petals, and a piece of paper. On the piece of paper, write down the conflict you wish to resolve and the names of all involved parties. Light the white candle and place the paper beside it. Sprinkle the rose petals around the candle. Focus on your intention for the conflict to be resolved peacefully and fairly for all involved. Repeat the following incantation three times: "Peace and harmony, come to me now. Help us to resolve this conflict in a fair and just way, so mote it be." Allow the candle to burn down completely.

"Harmonious Communication" Spell

You will need: a green candle, lavender flowers, and a piece of paper. On the piece of paper, write down your intention for harmonious communication. Light the green candle and sprinkle the lavender flowers around it. Hold the paper in your hands and focus on your intention. Repeat the following incantation three times: "Peaceful words I now impart. Harmony flows from my heart. So mote it be." Allow the candle to burn down completely.

Communication Spell for Improved Relationships

Choose a green or pink candle to represent love and communication. Light the candle and hold it in front of you. Visualize improved communication and understanding in your relationships. Repeat this visualization for as long as you like, and then extinguish the candle. Repeat this spell as often as needed.

"Speak Your Truth" Spell

You will need: a white candle, rose petals, and a pen. On a piece of paper, write down what you want to communicate and light the white candle. Sprinkle the rose petals around the candle. Hold the paper in your hands and focus on your intention to communicate clearly and effectively. Repeat the following incantation three times: "My words are clear, my voice is strong. I speak my truth and do no wrong. So mote it be." Allow the candle to burn down completely.

"Clear Communication" Spell

You will need: a blue candle, rosemary, and a piece of paper. On the piece of paper, write down your intention for clear communication. Light the blue candle and sprinkle the rosemary around it. Hold the paper in your hands and focus on your intention. Repeat the following incantation three times: "Clarity shines, confusion flees. Clear communication is what I need. So mote it be." Allow the candle to burn down completely.

Spell for Understanding

You will need: a white candle, a piece of paper, and rosemary. Write down your intention for understanding on the piece of paper. Light the white candle and sprinkle the rosemary around it. Hold the piece of paper in your hands and focus on your intention. Repeat the following incantation three times: "I call upon the power of understanding, help me to see clearly and to grasp the truth of the matter, so mote it be." Allow the candle to burn down completely.

Communication Spell for Better Expressing Yourself

Choose a green or pink candle to represent love and communication. Light the candle and hold it in front of you. Visualize better expression of your thoughts and feelings in communication with others. Repeat this visualization for as long as you like, and then extinguish the candle. Repeat this spell as often as needed.

"Effective Communication" Spell

You will need: a purple candle, basil, and a piece of paper. On the piece of paper, write down your intention for effective communication. Light the purple candle and sprinkle the basil around it. Hold the paper in your hands and focus on your intention. Repeat the following incantation three times: "Effective communication is my right. My words are powerful, my voice is bright. So mote it be." Allow the candle to burn down completely.

Communication Spell for Improved Writing Skills

You will need: a pen, a piece of paper, and lavender. Write down your intention for improved writing skills on the piece of paper. Light a piece of lavender and hold it in your left hand. Hold the piece of paper in your right hand and focus on your intention. Repeat the following incantation three times: "Words flow from me, my writing skills improve. I write with ease and my writing brings joy. So mote it be." Fold the paper and place it in a safe place. Use the pen to draw a pentacle on the piece of paper. Repeat this spell every day until you notice an improvement in your writing skills. *This spell is best performed during the waxing moon, when the energy is building towards a full moon and is believed to be favorable for spells related to growth and improvement.*

Spell for Improved Listening Skills

You will need: a yellow candle, a piece of paper, and rose petals. Write down your intention for improved listening skills on the piece of paper. Light the yellow candle and sprinkle the rose petals around it. Hold the piece of paper in your hands and focus on your intention. Repeat the following incantation three times: "Ears that listen, heart that hears, may my listening skills improve with each passing year. Help me to listen more deeply and understand more completely, so mote it be." Allow the candle to burn down completely.

Communication Spell for Improved Public Speaking

Choose a green or pink candle to represent love and communication. Light the candle and hold it in front of you. Visualize improved public speaking skills and successful communication in front of an audience. Repeat this visualization for as long as you like, and then extinguish the candle. Repeat this spell as often as needed.

"Open Communication" Spell

You will need: a yellow candle, jasmine flowers, and a piece of paper. On the piece of paper, write down your intention for open communication. Light the yellow candle and sprinkle the jasmine flowers around it. Hold the paper in your hands and focus on your intention. Repeat the following incantation three times: "Open ears, open hearts, open minds. Communication flows, peace I find. So mote it be." Allow the candle to burn down completely.

Communication Spell for Improved Telepathic Skills

Choose a green or pink candle to represent love and communication. Light the candle and hold it in front of you. Visualize improved telepathic skills and successful communication through the mind. Repeat this visualization for as long as you like, and then extinguish the candle. Repeat this spell as often as needed.

Spells with Crystals

Crystals have been used for centuries for their energetic properties and have been believed to enhance the power of spells and rituals. Each crystal has a unique energy that can be harnessed for specific purposes, such as promoting love, protection, abundance, and more. To perform a spell using crystals, you can carry the crystal with you, place it in a specific location, or hold it while focusing your intention. Here are some spells that can be performed with crystals to bring peace, harmony, and positive energy into your life.

Clear Quartz for Clarity Spell

This spell requires a clear quartz crystal and a quiet, meditative space. Sit comfortably with the clear quartz crystal in your hand. Close your eyes and take deep breaths, focusing on increasing clarity and concentration. Visualize the clear quartz crystal clearing your mind, leaving you with newfound clarity and focus. Repeat the following affirmations: "I am clear and focused. I have the power to achieve my goals. Clear quartz, bring me clarity and success." Hold the clear quartz crystal to your forehead and continue to focus on your intentions for a few minutes before opening your eyes.

Jasper Stability Spell

You will need a jasper crystal, an orange candle, and a piece of orange cloth. Light the orange candle and place it on the orange cloth. Hold the jasper in your right hand and focus on your intention for stability. Repeat the following chant three times: "Jasper, bring stability to me. Let my life be balanced, let my path be steady." Leave the candle to burn out completely, and carry the jasper with you for stability.

Lapis Lazuli Communication Spell

You will need a lapis lazuli crystal, a blue candle, and a piece of blue cloth. Light the blue candle and place it on the blue cloth. Hold the lapis lazuli in your left hand and focus on your intention for communication. Repeat the following chant three times: "Lapis lazuli, bring communication to me. Let my words be clear, let my message be heard." Leave the candle to burn out completely, and carry the lapis lazuli with you for improved communication.

Amethyst Success Spell

You will need an amethyst crystal, a green candle, and a piece of green cloth. Light the green candle and place it on the green cloth. Hold the amethyst in your left hand and focus on your intention for success. Repeat the following chant three times: "Amethyst, bring success to me. Let my path be clear, let my goals be achieved." Leave the candle to burn out completely, and carry the amethyst with you to attract success.

Amethyst for Inner Peace Spell

This spell requires an amethyst crystal, a piece of purple cloth, and a quiet place to sit. Hold the amethyst crystal in your hand and close your eyes. Visualize yourself feeling calm and centered, surrounded by a peaceful aura. Repeat the following affirmation three times: "I am surrounded by inner peace, I am protected and calm, Amethyst bring peace to my mind and soul." Place the amethyst crystal on the purple cloth and meditate with it for 10-15 minutes.

Citrine for Abundance Spell

This spell requires a citrine crystal, a yellow candle, and a piece of yellow cloth. Light the yellow candle and place it on the yellow cloth. Hold the citrine crystal in your hand and focus on your intention for financial abundance. Visualize yourself receiving money and imagine the citrine symbolizing abundance and prosperity. Repeat the following affirmation three times: "Money flows to me, abundance grows for me. Citrine, bring me prosperity and success." Leave the candle to burn out completely.

Jasper for Protection Spell

This spell requires a jasper crystal, a brown candle, and a piece of brown cloth. Light the brown candle and place it on the brown cloth. Hold the jasper crystal in your hand and focus on your intention for protection and security. Visualize yourself surrounded by a protective shield and imagine the jasper symbolizing protection and grounding. Repeat the following affirmation three times: "I am protected, I am secure. Jasper, bring me safety and grounding." Leave the candle to burn out completely.

Obsidian for Release Spell

This spell requires an obsidian crystal, a black candle, and a piece of black cloth. Light the black candle and place it on the black cloth. Hold the obsidian crystal in your hand and focus on your intention for release and letting go. Visualize yourself releasing negative energy and imagine the obsidian symbolizing release and protection. Repeat the following affirmation three times: "I release, I let go. Obsidian, bring me protection and release." Leave the candle to burn out completely.

Amethyst for Stress Relief Spell

This spell requires an amethyst crystal and a quiet, calming space. Sit comfortably with the amethyst crystal in your hand. Close your eyes and take deep breaths, focusing on letting go of stress and anxiety. Visualize the amethyst crystal absorbing all negative energy, leaving you feeling calm and relaxed. Repeat the following affirmations: "I release all stress and anxiety. I am calm and at peace. Amethyst, bring me serenity and balance." Hold the amethyst crystal to your heart and continue to focus on your intentions for a few minutes before opening your eyes.

Rose Quartz for Love Spell

This spell requires a rose quartz crystal and a quiet, peaceful space. Sit comfortably with the rose quartz crystal in your hand. Close your eyes and take deep breaths, focusing on attracting love and positive relationships. Visualize the rose quartz crystal spreading love and positive energy, bringing you closer to the love you desire. Repeat the following affirmations: "I am open to love and positive relationships. I am surrounded by love and positivity. Rose quartz, bring me love and happiness." Hold the rose quartz crystal to your heart and continue to focus on your intentions for a few minutes before opening your eyes.

Black Tourmaline for Protection Spell

This spell requires a black tourmaline crystal and a quiet, protected space. Sit comfortably with the black tourmaline crystal in your hand. Close your eyes and take deep breaths, focusing on protection and security. Visualize the black tourmaline crystal absorbing all negative energy, creating a protective barrier around you. Repeat the following affirmations: "I am protected and secure. No harm can come to me. Black tourmaline, bring me protection and peace." Hold the black tourmaline crystal to your heart and continue to focus on your intentions for a few minutes before opening your eyes.

Good Luck Spells

Good luck spells are a type of magic that is used to bring good fortune and positive energy into a person's life. These spells can be performed for a variety of purposes, such as to help with job interviews, to attract abundance, or to find love. Good luck spells can be performed with candles, crystals, herbs, and other materials, and they can be accompanied by affirmations, visualization, or ritual actions to amplify their energy and intention. Some common ingredients used in good luck spells include cinnamon, cloves, basil, lemon, and rose petals, which are believed to attract prosperity and success. Whether you are seeking a change in your financial situation, career, or love life, good luck spells can help you manifest your desires and attract the positive outcomes you are seeking.

Green Candle Good Luck Spell

Light a green candle and focus on your intention for good luck. Close your eyes and visualize a bright green light surrounding you, filling you with positive energy and good fortune. Repeat affirmations of your desired outcome, such as "I am worthy of good luck and success." Keep the candle burning for as long as you like, or until it burns out on its own. Repeat this spell as often as you need to boost your good luck energy.

Good Luck Herbs Spell

Choose herbs associated with good luck, such as basil, lavender, or rosemary. Create a small bundle of the herbs, tie it with a ribbon, and carry it with you, or place it in a special place where you will see it often. As you hold the herbs, focus on your intention for good luck and repeat affirmations, such as "Good luck is always with me." For best results, repeat this spell daily or as often as you need a boost of good luck energy. Remember to always believe in your own abilities and to have faith in the positive outcomes that you hope to achieve.

Good Luck Tea Spell

Brew a cup of tea with ingredients associated with good luck, such as chamomile, lemon, or mint. As you drink the tea, focus on your intention for good luck and repeat affirmations, such as "I am surrounded by good luck and positivity." Finish the cup of tea, and dispose of the remaining tea and ingredients in a way that feels respectful to you. Repeat this spell as often as you need a boost of good luck energy.

The Four Leaf Clover Charm

 For this spell, you will need a real or artificial four leaf clover. If you are using a real one, preserve it in resin or laminate it to make it last longer. Keep the clover with you at all times, either in your pocket, purse, or on a piece of jewelry. The four leaves represent hope, faith, love, and luck. As you carry the clover with you, visualize yourself surrounded by good luck and positive energy. Repeat positive affirmations to yourself, such as "I am worthy of good luck" and "Good things come my way."

Crystals for Good Luck

Choose a crystal that resonates with good luck, such as citrine, tiger's eye, or jade. Carry the crystal with you, place it in your pocket, or keep it in a special place where you will see it often. Focus on the crystal and visualize it amplifying your good luck energy. Repeat affirmations of your desired outcome, such as "I am attracting good luck and success." Repeat this spell as often as you need a boost of good luck energy.

The Candles and Herbs

For this spell, you will need a green candle and a combination of lucky herbs, such as basil, rosemary, and mint. Light the green candle and place it on a plate. Sprinkle the herbs around the candle and focus your intention on attracting good luck and prosperity. Repeat positive affirmations, such as "I am open to receiving good luck and abundance" and "My life is filled with prosperity and success." Leave the candle and herbs in place for as long as you like, and then extinguish the candle and dispose of the herbs when you are finished.

Salt for Good Luck

Sprinkle salt in the corners of your home or work space, or in any area where you want to attract good luck. As you sprinkle the salt, focus on your intention for good luck and repeat affirmations, such as "Good luck and positivity flow into my life." Leave the salt in place, or dispose of it in a way that feels respectful to you. Repeat this spell as often as you need a boost of good luck energy.

Lucky Charm Spell

To perform this spell, choose a lucky charm that resonates with you such as a horseshoe, a four-leaf clover, or a rabbit's foot. Cleanse the charm and charge it with your intention by holding it in both hands and focusing your energy into it. Repeat a mantra or affirmation to yourself such as "I am worthy of good luck and fortune." Keep the charm with you or place it in a prominent place in your home to attract good luck and positive energy.

The Crystal Grid

For this spell, you will need a clear quartz crystal and a green aventurine crystal. Place the clear quartz in the center of your grid and surround it with the green aventurine crystals in a circular pattern. Light a green candle and focus your intention on attracting good luck and prosperity. Repeat positive affirmations, such as "I am open to receiving good luck and abundance" and "My life is filled with prosperity and success." Leave the grid in place for as long as you like, and then dismantle it when you feel that the spell has done its job.

Good Luck Incense Spell

Burn incense associated with good luck, such as sandalwood, jasmine, or cinnamon. As the incense burns, focus on your intention for good luck and repeat affirmations, such as "Good luck and success come to me easily." Keep the incense burning for as long as you like, or until it burns out on its own. Repeat this spell as often as you need a boost of good luck energy.

Four Leaf Clover Spell

Find a real or symbolic four-leaf clover and carry it with you or place it in a special place where you will see it often. As you look at the clover, focus on your intention for good luck and repeat affirmations, such as "Good luck follows me wherever I go." Repeat this spell as often as you need a boost of good luck energy.

The Lucky Mojo Bag

For this spell, you will need a small cloth bag, a green or gold ribbon, and a combination of lucky items, such as a four leaf clover, a rabbit's foot, a penny, and a small piece of green aventurine. Place the items in the bag and tie it closed with the ribbon. Carry the bag with you at all times, either in your pocket, purse, or on a piece of jewelry. Repeat positive affirmations, such as "I am surrounded by good luck and positive energy" and "Good things come my way."

The Salt Bath

Fill a bathtub with warm water and add a handful of salt. As you soak in the bath, visualize yourself surrounded by good luck and positive energy. Repeat positive affirmations, such as "I am worthy of good luck" and "Good things come my way." Soak in the bath for as long as you like, and then drain the water when you are finished.

Prayer Spell

Take a moment to pray for good luck and prosperity in your life. This can be done in any way that feels meaningful to you, whether it's through a formal prayer or simply speaking from your heart. Repeat this prayer as often as you like, and remember to be grateful for the good luck and positive energy that comes into your life.

The Chanting

For this spell, you will need to choose a positive and empowering mantra, such as "good luck comes to me easily and effortlessly" or "I am worthy of good luck and abundance." Stand in front of a green or gold candle and light it. Repeat the mantra to yourself as you focus your intention on attracting good luck and prosperity. Repeat the mantra for as long as you like, and then extinguish the candle when you are finished.

Penny Spell

Find a penny and cleanse it by washing it in salt water. Hold the penny in your hands and focus on your intention for good luck. Repeat a mantra or affirmation such as "I attract good luck and prosperity into my life." Place the penny in your pocket or purse and keep it with you throughout the day. You can also place the penny in a special spot in your home or office to attract good luck and positive energy.

Good Fortune Candle Spell

Choose a green or gold candle to represent good fortune. Light the candle and place it in a safe place. Sit in front of the candle and visualize yourself surrounded by good luck and prosperity. Repeat this visualization for as long as you like, and then extinguish the candle. Repeat this spell as often as needed to attract good luck and positive energy into your life.

Rainbow Spell

On a sunny day, go outside and find a rainbow or create a symbolic rainbow. Stand facing the rainbow and focus on your intention for good luck. Repeat a mantra or affirmation such as "Good luck and prosperity follow me wherever I go" or "Good luck is always within my reach". Take a moment to bask in the positive energy of the rainbow, and then continue on with your day, feeling confident and lucky.

Binding and Banishing Spells

Binding and Banishing Spells are powerful rituals used for a variety of purposes, including protection, release from negative energy or entities, and to bring about positive change in one's life. Binding spells are used to restrict or limit the actions or influence of a person, place, or thing. On the other hand, banishing spells are used to remove unwanted energy, people, or entities from your life. These spells require focus, intention, and often specific materials such as candles, herbs, and crystals. It is important to use caution when casting Binding and Banishing Spells, as they can have strong effects on both the caster and the target. As with all spell work, it is important to be clear on your intention and to only cast spells that align with your values and ethical principles.

Binding Spell for Negative Energy

Choose a black or red candle to represent banishing and protection. Light the candle and hold it in front of you. Visualize any negative energy being bound and unable to harm you. Repeat this visualization for as long as you like, and then extinguish the candle. Repeat this spell as often as needed.

Banishing Spell for Negative Thoughts

Write down any negative thoughts or worries that you have on a piece of paper. Fold the paper and place it in front of a black or red candle. Light the candle and visualize the negative thoughts being burned away and banished. Repeat this visualization for as long as you like, and then extinguish the candle. Keep the paper as a reminder of the banishment.

Binding Spell for Harmful People

Choose a black or red candle to represent banishing and protection. Light the candle and hold it in front of you. Visualize any harmful people being bound and unable to cause you harm. Repeat this visualization for as long as you like, and then extinguish the candle. Repeat this spell as often as needed.

Banishing Spell for Negative Situations

Write down any negative situations that you are facing on a piece of paper. Fold the paper and place it in front of a black or red candle. Light the candle and visualize the negative situations being burned away and banished. Repeat this visualization for as long as you like, and then extinguish the candle. Keep the paper as a reminder of the banishment.

Binding Spell for Addictions

Choose a black or red candle to represent banishing and protection. Light the candle and hold it in front of you. Visualize any addictions being bound and unable to control you. Repeat this visualization for as long as you like, and then extinguish the candle. Repeat this spell as often as needed.

Banishing Spell for Nightmares

Write down any nightmares or fears that you have on a piece of paper. Fold the paper and place it in front of a black or red candle. Light the candle and visualize the nightmares being burned away and banished. Repeat this visualization for as long as you like, and then extinguish the candle. Keep the paper as a reminder of the banishment.

Binding Spell for Negative Habits

Choose a black or red candle to represent banishing and protection. Light the candle and hold it in front of you. Visualize any negative habits being bound and unable to control you. Repeat this visualization for as long as you like, and then extinguish the candle. Repeat this spell as often as needed.

Banishing Spell for Unwanted Guests

Write down the names of any unwanted guests on a piece of paper. Fold the paper and place it in front of a black or red candle. Light the candle and visualize the unwanted guests being burned away and banished. Repeat this visualization for as long as you like, and then extinguish the candle. Keep the paper as a reminder of the banishment.

Binding Spell for Negative Energy in Objects

Choose a black or red candle to represent banishing and protection. Light the candle and hold it in front of you. Visualize any negative energy in objects being bound and unable to harm you. Repeat this visualization for as long as you like, and then extinguish the candle. Repeat this spell as often as needed.

Banishing Spell for Negative Memories

Write down any negative memories that you have on a piece of paper. Fold the paper and place it in front of a black or red candle. Light the candle and visualize the negative memories being burned away and banished. Repeat this visualization for as long as you like, and then extinguish the candle. Keep the paper as a reminder of the banishment.

Herbs Banishing Spell

Gather together basil, black pepper, and salt. Sprinkle them in a counter-clockwise circle around the area where you wish to banish negative energy. Repeat this three times, each time saying, "Negative energy, be gone from this place." Vacuum or sweep the area clean to remove the herbs.

Candle Banishing Spell

Light a black candle and place it in a holder. Stand before the candle and visualize all negative energy leaving your body and dissipating into the air. Repeat this visualization until the candle burns out. Discard the candle and holder.

Mirror Banishing Spell

Place a small, hand-held mirror on a table. Stand before the mirror and visualize all negative energy reflecting back to the sender. Repeat this visualization until you feel the negative energy has been neutralized. Store the mirror in a safe place.

Protection Circle Banishing Spell

Draw a protective circle using salt or chalk. Stand within the circle and visualize all negative energy being trapped outside the circle and unable to enter. Repeat this visualization until you feel the negative energy has been neutralized. Erase the circle when finished.

Elemental Banishing Spell

Call upon the elements of earth, air, fire, and water to banish negative energy. Light a green candle to represent earth, a yellow candle to represent air, a red candle to represent fire, and a blue candle to represent water. Focus your energy on each element in turn, asking for its assistance in banishing negative energy. Repeat this visualization until you feel the negative energy has been neutralized. Extinguish the candles when finished.

Smudging Banishing Spell

Light a sage smudge stick and waft the smoke around the area where you wish to banish negative energy. Repeat this visualization until you feel the negative energy has been neutralized. Extinguish the smudge stick.

Affirmation Banishing Spell

Stand before a mirror and repeat the following affirmation three times

"I banish all negative energy from my life. I am surrounded by love and positivity." Repeat this visualization until you feel the negative energy has been neutralized.

Bell Banishing Spell

Ring a bell three times in the area where you wish to banish negative energy. Visualize all negative energy being dispersed by the sound of the bell. Repeat this visualization until you feel the negative energy has been neutralized. Store the bell in a safe place.

Banishing Candle Spell

Light a black or red candle and hold it in your hand. Close your eyes and visualize any negative energy being absorbed into the flame. As you do this, repeat a phrase such as "I banish negativity and welcome positivity." When finished, blow out the candle.

Herbal Banishing Spell

Gather a handful of banishing herbs such as basil, sage, or rosemary. Light a charcoal disc and place the herbs on top. Focus your intention on banishing any negative energy and repeat a banishing incantation. When the herbs have burned down, dispose of the ashes outside.

Crystal Banishing Spell

Place a black tourmaline or obsidian crystal on your altar. Focus your intention on banishing negativity and imagine the crystal absorbing all negative energy. Repeat a banishing incantation and leave the crystal on your altar for as long as you feel necessary.

Salt Circle Banishing Spell

Draw a circle with salt around yourself or the object you wish to banish negativity from. Light a black or red candle and place it inside the circle. Focus your intention on banishing negativity and repeat a banishing incantation. When finished, blow out the candle and dispose of the salt.

Banishing Jar Spell

Fill a glass jar with banishing herbs, black tourmaline or obsidian crystals, and a piece of black or red cloth. Close the jar with a lid and focus your intention on banishing negativity. Repeat a banishing incantation and keep the jar in a safe place.

Banishing Bath Spell

Fill a bathtub with warm water and add banishing herbs such as basil, sage, or rosemary. Light candles and focus your intention on banishing negativity. Soak in the bath for as long as you like, and when finished, dispose of the water outside.

Banishing Smoke Spell

Light a smudge stick of sage or palo santo and walk around the area you wish to banish negativity from, wafting the smoke with your hand. Focus your intention on banishing negativity and repeat a banishing incantation. When finished, extinguish the smudge stick.

Banishing Chant Spell

Stand in a quiet place and focus your intention on banishing negativity. Repeat a banishing incantation or chant for as long as you feel necessary. When finished, take a deep breath and imagine all negative energy being expelled from your body.

Banishing Sigil Spell

Draw a banishing sigil on a piece of paper. Light a black or red candle and hold the paper in front of the flame. Focus your intention on banishing negativity and repeat a banishing incantation. When finished, burn the paper and dispose of the ashes.

Banishing Water Spell

Fill a bowl with water and add banishing herbs such as basil, sage, or rosemary. Light a black or red candle and place it next to the bowl. Focus your intention on banishing negativity and repeat a banishing incantation. When finished, pour the water outside.

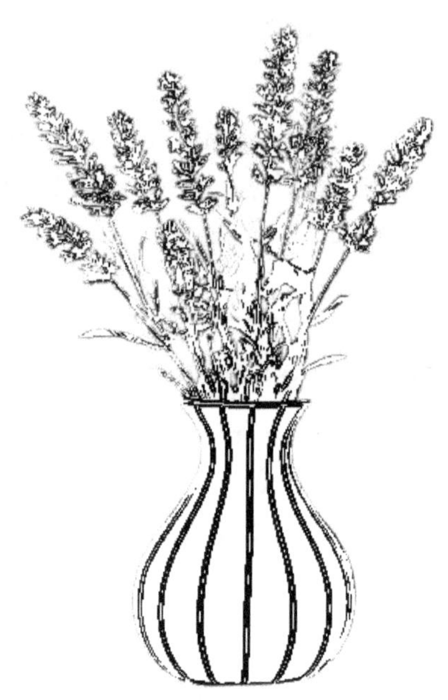

Clarity Spells

Clarity spells are used to gain a clearer understanding of a situation, person, or one's own thoughts and feelings. These spells help to remove confusion, negative energy, and obstacles that may be blocking one's path to clarity. The goal of clarity spells is to bring peace and balance to the mind, allowing one to make informed decisions and move forward with confidence. Clarity spells can involve the use of crystals, candles, affirmations, visualization, and other tools to help bring the desired outcome to fruition. Whether you are seeking clarity in your personal life, relationships, or career, a clarity spell can help to bring focus, peace, and understanding to your situation.

Spell for Mental Clarity

You will need: a clear quartz crystal, a green candle, and rosemary. Light the green candle and hold the clear quartz crystal in your hand. Repeat the following incantation three times: "Mental clarity, come to me now. Help me to see things clearly and make wise decisions, so mote it be." Sprinkle rosemary around the candle, and let it burn down completely.

Spell for Emotional Clarity

You will need: a blue candle, lavender, and a piece of paper. Write down your intention for emotional clarity on the piece of paper. Light the blue candle and sprinkle the lavender around it. Hold the piece of paper in your hands and focus on your intention. Repeat the following incantation three times: "Emotional clarity, come to me now. Help me to understand my emotions, so mote it be." Allow the candle to burn down completely.

Spell for Enhancing Creativity

You will need: a yellow candle, rose petals, and lavender. Find a quiet and comfortable space to perform the spell. Light the yellow candle and place the rose petals and lavender around it. Sit down in front of the candle and close your eyes. Take several deep breaths and focus on your intention to enhance your creativity. Repeat the following incantation three times: "Creativity, flow through me. Let my imagination soar, and my ideas take flight. So mote it be." Allow the candle to burn down completely.

Clarity Spell for Vision

You will need: a yellow candle, a piece of paper, and a pen. Write down your vision for the future on the piece of paper. Light the yellow candle and hold the piece of paper in your hands. Repeat the following incantation three times: "Clarity, come to me now. Help me to see my vision clearly, so mote it be." Allow the candle to burn down completely.

Spell for Clarity in Decision Making

You will need: a yellow candle, a piece of paper, and basil. Write down your intention for clarity in decision making on the piece of paper. Light the yellow candle and sprinkle the basil around it. Hold the piece of paper in your hands and focus on your intention. Repeat the following incantation three times: "Clarity in decision making, come to me now. Help me to choose wisely, so mote it be." Allow the candle to burn down completely.

Spell for Spiritual Clarity

You will need: a selenite crystal, a piece of sage, and a white candle. Light the white candle and sit quietly with the selenite crystal in your hand. Focus on your intention to achieve spiritual clarity and let go of any negative thoughts or distractions. Burn the piece of sage and repeat the following incantation three times: "I ask for spiritual clarity, for the ability to connect with my higher self and the universe. So mote it be." Hold the selenite crystal close to the sage smoke and allow the candle to burn down completely.

Spell for Career Clarity

You will need: a blue candle, a piece of paper, and lavender. Write down your career goals on the piece of paper. Light the blue candle and sprinkle the lavender around it. Hold the piece of paper in your hands and focus on your career goals. Repeat the following incantation three times: "Clarity in my career, guide me true. Help me to achieve my goals, so mote it be." Allow the candle to burn down completely.

Spell for Improving Focus

You will need: a blue candle, rosemary, and a piece of rose quartz. Light the blue candle and place the rosemary and rose quartz near it. Sit down in front of the candle and close your eyes. Hold the rose quartz in your hand and repeat the following incantation three times: "Focus, be mine. Help me to concentrate and stay on task. Let my mind be clear and my thoughts be sharp. So mote it be." Allow the candle to burn down completely.

Spell for Clarity in Communication

You will need: an orange candle, a piece of paper, and mint. Write down your intention for clarity in communication on the piece of paper. Light the orange candle and sprinkle the mint around it. Hold the piece of paper in your hands and focus on your intention. Repeat the following incantation three times: "Clarity in communication, come to me now. Help me to be understood, so mote it be." Allow the candle to burn down completely.

Spell for Clarity in Relationships

You will need: a pink candle, a piece of paper, and jasmine. Write down your relationship goals on the piece of paper. Light the pink candle and sprinkle the jasmine around it. Hold the piece of paper in your hands and focus on your relationship goals. Repeat the following incantation three times: "Clarity in my relationships, help me see. Guide me to the right path, so mote it be." Allow the candle to burn down completely.

Spell for Clearing Negative Energy

You will need: a white candle, salt, and sage. Start by casting a circle of salt around the area where you will be performing the spell. Light the white candle and hold the sage in your dominant hand. Wave the sage around the candle, and as you do, repeat the following incantation: "Negative energy, be gone. I release all that does not serve me. May only positivity and clarity remain." Continue to wave the sage around the candle for as long as you feel is necessary. When you are done, allow the candle to burn down completely and dispose of the sage and any remaining salt in a way that feels appropriate to you.

Good Fortune Spells

Good fortune spells are designed to help bring prosperity, abundance, and success into your life. These spells can be performed using a variety of tools and ingredients, such as candles, incense, crystals, herbs, and affirmations. The goal of good fortune spells is to attract positive energy and release any negative energy or blockages that may be hindering your success. They can be used to manifest abundance in any area of life, such as finances, career, love, or health. When casting a good fortune spell, it is important to focus on the desired outcome and to have faith in the power of magic. Whether you are looking to attract more money, find a new job, or improve your relationships, a good fortune spell can help you manifest the life you desire.

Spell for Abundance and Prosperity

You will need: a green candle, cinnamon, nutmeg, and a piece of paper. Write down your intention for abundance and prosperity on the piece of paper. Light the green candle and sprinkle the cinnamon and nutmeg around it. Hold the piece of paper in your hands and focus on your intention. Repeat the following incantation three times: "Prosperity and abundance, come to me now. Fill my life with all that I need, so mote it be." Allow the candle to burn down completely.

Spell for Happiness and Joy

You will need: a pink candle, a piece of paper, and lavender. Write down your intention for happiness and joy on the piece of paper. Light the pink candle and sprinkle the lavender around it. Hold the piece of paper in your hands and focus on your intention. Repeat the following incantation three times: "Happiness and joy, come to me now. Help me to live a life filled with love and light, so mote it be." Allow the candle to burn down completely.

"Gratitude Jar" Spell

You will need: a clear glass jar, colorful stones, and small pieces of paper. On each piece of paper, write down one thing that you are grateful for. Fold the papers and place them in the jar. Add the colorful stones to the jar, filling it up as much as possible. Place the jar in a prominent place in your home, and whenever you feel down, reach for it and read one of the papers. The energy of gratitude will bring more good fortune into your life.

Spell for Wealth and Success

You will need: a green candle, a piece of paper, and basil. Write down your intention for wealth and success on the piece of paper. Light the green candle and sprinkle the basil around it. Hold the piece of paper in your hands and focus on your intention. Repeat the following incantation three times: "Wealth and success, come to me now. Help me to achieve my goals, so mote it be." Allow the candle to burn down completely.

Spell for Opportunity

You will need: a yellow candle, a piece of paper, a pen, and rosemary. Write down your intention for opportunity on the piece of paper. Light the yellow candle and sprinkle the rosemary around it. Hold the piece of paper in your hands and focus on your intention. Repeat the following incantation three times: "Opportunities, come to me now. Bring growth and success, so mote it be." Allow the candle to burn down completely.

"Hand of Fatima" Spell

You will need: a piece of blue or green string, and your left hand. Take the string and make a loop that fits snugly over your left thumb. Take the ends of the string and cross them over the back of your hand, then bring them back around to the front and cross them again over your thumb. Repeat this process until you have created a web-like pattern over your hand. Repeat the following incantation three times: "Prosperity, success, and good fortune come to me now. The Hand of Fatima protects and brings me blessings, so mote it be." Wear the string on your left hand as a symbol of good fortune.

"Prosperity Stones" Spell

You will need: a handful of green aventurine stones and a quiet place to meditate. Close your eyes and hold the stones in your hands. Visualize yourself surrounded by abundance, wealth, and prosperity. Repeat the following incantation three times: "Prosperity, abundance, wealth come to me now. Bring me good fortune, so mote it be." Carry the stones with you wherever you go, and feel the energy of prosperity surrounding you.

Spell for Career Success

You will need: a yellow candle, bay leaves, and a piece of paper. Write down your intention for career success on the piece of paper. Light the yellow candle and place the bay leaves around it. Hold the piece of paper in your hands and focus on your intention. Repeat the following incantation three times: "Career success, come to me now. Help me to succeed in all that I do, so mote it be." Allow the candle to burn down completely.

Spell for Good Luck

You will need: a small piece of green cloth, a small piece of paper, a pen, and three coins. Write your intention for good luck on the piece of paper. Place the coins and the paper inside the green cloth, and tie it closed. Carry the tied cloth with you, and touch it every time you need a boost of good luck.

Spell for Financial Stability

You will need: a green candle, a piece of paper, and cinnamon. Write down your intention for financial stability on the piece of paper. Light the green candle and sprinkle the cinnamon around it. Hold the piece of paper in your hands and focus on your intention. Repeat the following incantation three times: "Financial stability, come to me now. Help me to achieve financial independence, so mote it be." Allow the candle to burn down completely.

Blessing and Purification Spells

Blessing and purification spells are rituals and incantations used to cleanse negative energy and promote positivity and good luck. These spells often involve the use of symbolic elements such as sage, salt, and holy water to clear out any unwanted energy and create a space of peace and calm. The spells can also include affirmations and visualizations to focus one's intentions and attract blessings into their life. They can be performed on people, objects, or even homes to bring in positivity, purify the surroundings, and create a peaceful environment. Blessing and purification spells are often used before other spells or rituals to create a clean and clear foundation for positive energy to flow into.

Blessing of the Home

To perform this spell, gather white candles, a feather, and salt. Light the candles and sprinkle salt in each room of your home, starting from the front door and working your way clockwise. As you sprinkle the salt, visualize any negativity being drawn out and dissipated. Once you've finished, use the feather to waft the smoke of the candles throughout the home, saying: "I bless this home and all within it. May peace, love, and positivity abound."

Purification Bath

Fill a bathtub with warm water and add a handful of sea salt. Light candles and incense, and place them near the bathtub. Soak in the bath for 20 minutes, visualizing any negative energy being washed away and purified. When you're finished, drain the water and repeat the process with fresh water and salt.

Smudging Ritual

Light a sage stick or palo santo, and use it to waft smoke throughout your home, starting from the front door and working your way clockwise. As you move, visualize any negative energy being dispersed and purified. Repeat this process until you feel that the space is cleansed.

Chakra Cleansing

Lie down in a quiet, dark room, and visualize a white light starting at the crown of your head. As you breathe deeply, visualize the white light flowing down through each of your chakras, clearing and purifying each one. Repeat this visualization until you feel that each chakra is clear and balanced.

"Blessing and Purification Chanting" Spell

You will need: a quiet place to sit and meditate. Sit in a comfortable position and begin to breathe deeply and slowly. Repeat the following incantation three times, focusing on your intention to purify and bless your body and spirit: "I purify and bless this body and spirit. May negativity be removed and positivity be embraced. So mote it be." When you are finished, take a few deep breaths and release any remaining tension in your body.

"Blessing and Purification Bath" Spell

You will need: sea salt, lavender essential oil, and a bathtub or basin. Fill the bathtub or basin with warm water and add a cup of sea salt. Stir the salt into the water with your hand to dissolve it. Add 5-7 drops of lavender essential oil to the water and stir it in with your hand. Climb into the bathtub or basin and soak in the water for 20-30 minutes, focusing on your intention to purify and bless your body and spirit. When you are finished, drain the water and rinse your body with clean water.

Blessing and Purification Room Spray

You will need a spray bottle, distilled water, and a blend of essential oils such as lavender, rosemary, and eucalyptus. Fill the spray bottle with distilled water and add several drops of the essential oil blend. Shake well and spray the mist around the room. Repeat the following incantation: "With this spray, I bless and purify this space. May all negativity be dispelled and may only positive energy remain. So mote it be."

Herb Blessing

Choose a mixture of herbs that resonate with you, such as lavender, rose petals, or chamomile. Create a small, loose bundle of the herbs and tie it with a white ribbon. Hold the bundle in both hands and bless it with your intention, saying something like

"May this herb bundle bring peace, love, and positivity to all who use it." Place the bundle in a small, decorative bag, and use it to bless your home or objects, or to carry with you for protection.

"Blessing and Purification Smudging" Spell

You will need: sage, a feather, and a fireproof dish. Light the sage and use the feather to waft the smoke over your body and around the space in which you are performing the spell. Repeat the following incantation as you smudge: "I purify and bless this body and space. May negativity be removed and positivity be embraced. So mote it be." When you are finished, blow out the sage and dispose of it in a fireproof dish.

New Moon Spells

New Moon spells are rituals and affirmations performed during the new moon phase to harness the energy and potential of this time. The new moon is a time of new beginnings and fresh starts, making it an ideal time to set intentions and start new projects. When working with the energy of the new moon, it is important to focus on what you want to bring into your life and to let go of what no longer serves you. This can be done through visualization, meditation, or written affirmations. Some popular New Moon spells include spells for manifestation, spells for self-discovery, and spells for letting go. To enhance the spell, you can also use crystals, candles, and essential oils that correspond with your intention. Whether you are looking to manifest abundance, find inner peace, or start a new chapter in your life, New Moon spells can help you tap into the power of the cosmos and bring your desires to fruition.

Spell to Release Negative Energy

This spell is best performed during a new moon as a way to start fresh and release any negativity that may be holding you back. You will need a black candle, sage, and a lighter. Start by lighting the sage and using it to cleanse your space. Light the black candle and focus on your intention to release negative energy. Repeat the following incantation three times: "By the power of the new moon, I release all negative energy. So be it." After repeating the incantation, visualize the negative energy leaving your body and dissipating into the air. Allow the candle to burn down completely and then dispose of it.

New Moon Prosperity Spell

Gather a green candle, some rose petals, and a piece of citrine. Place the candle in a safe holder and light it. Sprinkle the rose petals around the candle. Hold the citrine in your hands and visualize abundance and prosperity flowing into your life. Repeat the following incantation three times: "By the power of the new moon, I call forth abundance and prosperity. So be it." Allow the candle to burn out completely.

New Moon Gratitude Spell

This spell is designed to help you tap into the energy of the new moon to focus on gratitude and abundance. You will need a green candle, a piece of paper and pen, and matches or a lighter. On the piece of paper, write down a list of things you are grateful for and things you want to manifest in your life. Light the green candle and hold the piece of paper in front of the flame. Repeat the following incantation three times: "By the light of the new moon, I manifest abundance and gratitude. So be it." Allow the candle to burn down completely and then keep the piece of paper as a reminder of your intentions.

Spell to Improve Relationships

This spell is ideal for those looking to improve their relationships during a new moon. You will need a pink candle, rose petals, and matches or a lighter. Light the pink candle and sprinkle rose petals around it. Repeat the following incantation three times: "By the power of the new moon, I improve my relationships. So be it." Allow the candle to burn down completely and focus on the energy of love and positivity as it permeates your relationships.

New Moon Intentions Spell

Light a white candle and sit in a quiet, peaceful place. Close your eyes and take several deep breaths. Think about your intentions for the coming month and write them down on a piece of paper. Hold the paper in your hands and visualize your intentions coming true. Repeat the following incantation three times: "By the light of the new moon, I set my intentions, may they manifest in the coming month." Blow out the candle and keep the piece of paper in a safe place until the next full moon.

New Moon Protection Spell

Gather a blue candle, some salt, and a piece of black tourmaline. Place the candle in a safe holder and light it. Sprinkle the salt around the candle. Hold the black tourmaline in your hands and visualize yourself surrounded by a protective shield. Repeat the following incantation three times: "By the power of the new moon, I call forth protection, may I be safe and secure." Allow the candle to burn out completely.

New Moon Career Spell

For this spell, you will need a green candle, a piece of paper, a pen, and any herbs or crystals that you associate with career success and prosperity (such as basil, mint, rosemary, citrine, or garnet). Begin by lighting the green candle and sitting quietly for a few moments to focus your mind and clear your thoughts. On the piece of paper, write down your career aspirations and any specific goals that you would like to manifest.

Next, sprinkle the herbs or crystals around the candle, and hold the paper in your hands. Close your eyes and visualize your career goals coming to fruition. See yourself in a successful, fulfilling job, surrounded by abundance and prosperity. Repeat the following incantation three times: "With the power of this new moon, I call forth a successful and prosperous career. May my skills and talents be recognized and rewarded, so mote it be."

Allow the candle to burn down completely, and carry the piece of paper with you or place it somewhere where you will see it often as a reminder of your intentions. Repeat this spell during each new moon to continue to build and reinforce your manifestation power.

New Moon Releasing Spell

For this spell, you will need a piece of paper and a pen, as well as a lighter or matches. On the night of the new moon, write down any negative thoughts, patterns, or behaviors that you would like to release from your life. Fold the paper in half and light it with the lighter or matches, allowing it to burn completely. Repeat the following affirmation: "With the power of this new moon, I release all negative energy and welcome positivity into my life."

New Moon Healing Spell

Gather a yellow candle, some lavender, and a piece of amethyst. Place the candle in a safe holder and light it. Sprinkle the lavender around the candle. Hold the amethyst in your hands and visualize yourself being surrounded by healing energy. Repeat the following incantation three times: "By the power of the new moon, I call forth healing, may I be whole and well." Allow the candle to burn out completely.

New Moon Manifestation Spell

To perform this spell, you'll need a piece of paper and a pen, as well as a small dish of salt. On the night of the new moon, write down your goals and desires for the upcoming month. Sprinkle a small amount of salt over the paper and say the following affirmation: "With the power of this new moon, I manifest my desires and bring them into reality." Fold the paper in half and place it in a safe, dark place, such as a drawer or box.

New Moon Release Spell

Light a black candle and sit in a quiet, peaceful place. Close your eyes and take several deep breaths. Think about any negative energy, emotions, or habits that you would like to release. Write them down on a piece of paper. Hold the paper in your hands and visualize the negative energy leaving your body. Repeat the following incantation three times: "By the light of the new moon, I release what no longer serves me, may I be free of it." Burn the piece of paper in the flame of the black candle.

New Moon Happiness Spell

To perform this spell, you'll need a piece of paper and a pen, as well as a white candle. On the night of the new moon, write down a list of things you are grateful for in your life. Light the white candle and sit quietly, focusing your thoughts on gratitude and positivity. Repeat the following affirmation three times: "With the power of this new moon, I give thanks for all the blessings in my life and attract even more abundance and happiness."

Spell to Reinvent Yourself

This spell is ideal for a new moon as it is a time of new beginnings and transformation. You will need a yellow candle, a piece of paper and pen, and matches or a lighter. On the piece of paper, write down the traits or habits you wish to change about yourself. Light the yellow candle and hold the piece of paper in front of the flame. Repeat the following incantation three times: "By the power of the new moon, I reinvent myself. So be it." Allow the candle to burn down completely and then keep the piece of paper as a reminder of your intentions.

New Moon Love Spell

Light a pink candle and sit in a quiet, peaceful place. Close your eyes and take several deep breaths. Think about love and what you would like to attract into your life. Write your desires down on a piece of paper. Hold the paper in your hands and visualize yourself surrounded by love and happiness. Repeat the following incantation three times: "By the light of the new moon, I call forth love and happiness, may it come to me." Keep the piece of paper in a safe place until the next full moon.

Moonlit Abundance Spell

To perform this spell, you'll need a green candle, a piece of paper and a pen. Light the green candle and sit quietly for a few moments, focusing your thoughts on abundance and prosperity. On the piece of paper, write a list of all the things you would like to manifest in your life, including financial abundance, success, happiness, and love. When you have finished your list, fold the paper in half and hold it over the flame of the green candle, allowing it to catch fire. Hold it until the fire burns out, then allow the ashes to fall into a nearby dish. Repeat the following affirmation: "With the power of this new moon, I call forth abundance and prosperity into my life."

New Moon Wishing Spell

For this spell, you will need a piece of paper and a pen. On the night of the new moon, sit in a quiet place where you will not be disturbed. Write down your wishes for the upcoming month, being as specific as possible. Fold the paper in half and hold it to your chest while you close your eyes and repeat the following affirmation three times: "With the power of this new moon, I call forth my desires and dreams. So be it." Keep the paper in a safe place, and allow the energy of the new moon to work its magic.

Spell to Find Inner Peace

This spell is perfect for those seeking peace and tranquility during a new moon. You will need a white candle, lavender oil, and matches or a lighter. Light the white candle and place a few drops of lavender oil on your temples and pulse points. Close your eyes and focus on your breath. Repeat the following incantation three times: "By the grace of the new moon, I find inner peace. So be it." Allow the candle to burn down completely and continue to focus on your breath and the sensations of peace and tranquility.

Waxing Moon Spells

Waxing Moon Spells are spells that are performed during the waxing phase of the moon, which is the period between the New Moon and the Full Moon. The waxing moon is associated with growth and increase, making it an ideal time to cast spells for manifestation, abundance, and personal development. During this phase, the moon's energy is growing and increasing, making it a powerful time to cast spells for attracting positive energy, prosperity, and success into your life. When performing waxing moon spells, it is important to focus your intentions on growth, abundance, and manifestation, and to use crystals and other tools that are associated with these energies. Some popular crystals for waxing moon spells include Citrine, Moonstone, and Clear Quartz, as these stones are believed to help amplify the energy of the waxing moon and bring good fortune and abundance into your life.

Enhance Creativity Spell

Gather a yellow candle, a piece of paper, a pen, and some lavender. Write down your intention for enhancing your creativity on the piece of paper. Light the yellow candle and sprinkle the lavender around it. Hold the paper in both hands and visualize your creativity flowing freely as you repeat the following words: "Creativity, come to me. I am open and inspired. So mote it be." Let the candle burn down completely.

Attract Abundance Spell

To perform this spell, gather a green candle, some mint leaves, a coin, and a piece of paper. Write down your intention for attracting abundance on the piece of paper. Light the green candle and sprinkle the mint leaves around it. Hold the coin in your dominant hand and visualize abundance flowing into your life as you repeat the following words: "Money, come to me, in abundance three times three. So mote it be." Place the coin on top of the paper and let the candle burn down completely.

Manifesting Abundance Spell

To perform this spell, you will need a green candle, a piece of paper, and a pen. Light the green candle and hold the piece of paper in front of you. Close your eyes and focus on your intention to manifest abundance in your life. When you feel ready, write down all of the things that you desire to have abundance in, such as your finances, health, relationships, and career. Fold the piece of paper and place it under the candle. Repeat the following affirmation: "I attract abundance and prosperity in all areas of my life." Allow the candle to burn down completely.

Increasing Success Spell

For this spell, you will need an orange candle, a citrine crystal, and some cinnamon sticks. Light the orange candle and hold the citrine crystal in your hand. Close your eyes and focus on your intention to increase your success in life. Visualize yourself as successful and thriving in all areas of your life. Sprinkle the cinnamon sticks around the candle and repeat the following affirmation: "I am successful and thriving in all areas of my life." Allow the candle to burn down completely.

Find Love Spell

For this spell, you'll need a pink candle, rose petals, a piece of paper, and a pen. Write your name and the name of the person you'd like to attract into your life on the piece of paper. Sprinkle the rose petals around the pink candle and light it. Hold the paper in both hands and visualize love and happiness as you say the following words: "Love, come to me. I am open and ready. So mote it be." Let the candle burn down completely.

Improve Communication Spell

For this spell, you'll need a blue candle, some rosemary, a piece of paper, and a pen. Write down your intention for improving your communication skills on the piece of paper. Light the blue candle and sprinkle the rosemary around it. Hold the paper in both hands and visualize clear and effective communication as you repeat the following words: "Communication, come to me. I am heard and understood. So mote it be." Let the candle burn down completely.

Boost Confidence Spell

Gather an orange candle, a piece of paper, a pen, and some basil. Write down your intention for boosting your confidence on the piece of paper. Light the orange candle and sprinkle the basil around it. Hold the paper in both hands and visualize yourself radiating confidence as you repeat the following words: "Confidence, come to me. I am strong and self-assured. So mote it be." Let the candle burn down completely.

Attracting Love Spell

For this spell, you will need a pink candle, a rose quartz crystal, and some rose petals. Light the pink candle and hold the rose quartz crystal in your hand. Close your eyes and focus on your intention to attract love into your life. Visualize yourself surrounded by love and happiness. Sprinkle the rose petals around the candle and repeat the following affirmation: "I am open to love and happiness in my life." Allow the candle to burn down completely.

Self Assurance Spell

For this spell, you will need a yellow candle, a tiger's eye crystal, and some rosemary leaves. Light the yellow candle and hold the tiger's eye crystal in your hand. Close your eyes and focus on your intention to boost your confidence. Visualize yourself as confident and self-assured. Sprinkle the rosemary leaves around the candle and repeat the following affirmation: "I am confident and self-assured in all areas of my life." Allow the candle to burn down completely.

Banishing Negativity Spell

For this spell, you will need a black candle, a piece of black tourmaline, and some sage leaves. Light the black candle and hold the black tourmaline in your hand. Close your eyes and focus on your intention to banish negativity from your life. Visualize yourself surrounded by positive energy and light. Sprinkle the sage leaves around the candle and repeat the following affirmation: "I banish negativity and welcome positivity into my life." Allow the candle to burn down completely.

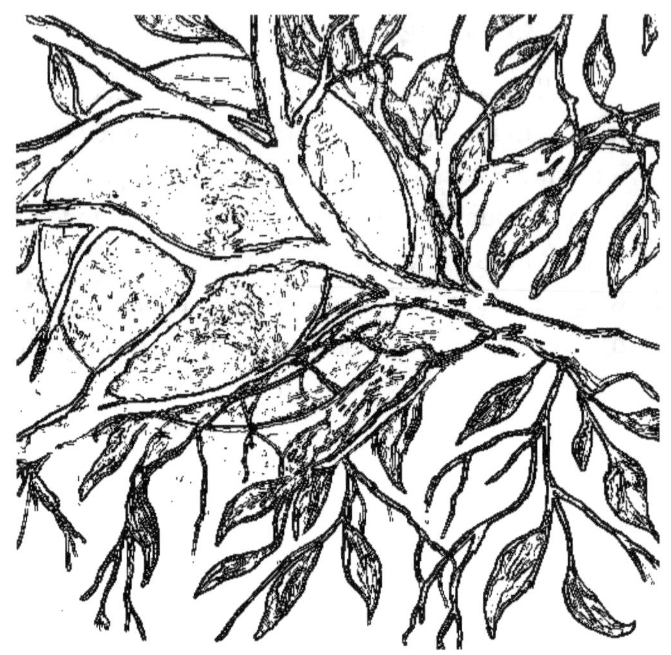

Full Moon Spells

Full Moon spells are powerful rituals that are performed during the time of the full moon. This phase is considered to be a time of manifestation, when wishes and desires can be amplified and brought to fruition. Full Moon spells can be used for a variety of purposes, from attracting love and abundance to releasing negative energy and promoting inner peace. Some common ingredients used in Full Moon spells include candles, herbs, crystals, and moon water. These rituals can be performed alone or in a group, and can be as simple or elaborate as you like. To perform a Full Moon spell, it is important to focus on your intention and be mindful of the energy that you are calling forth. This type of spell can be a powerful tool for manifesting your desires and creating the life that you want.

Full Moon Gratitude Spell

Write down 10 things you are grateful for on a piece of paper and place it outside during the full moon. As you gaze at the full moon, take a deep breath and visualize yourself becoming more and more grateful for these things. Repeat the following chant three times: "Full moon, bring me health and happiness. Fill me with gratitude, prosperity, and success."

Full Moon Healing Spell:

Write down the areas of your life that you would like to heal on a piece of paper and place it outside during the full moon. As you gaze at the full moon, take a deep breath and visualize yourself becoming more and more healed in these areas. Repeat the following chant three times: "Full moon, heal my mind, body, and spirit. Bring me peace, joy, and harmony."

Full Moon Love Spell

Write down the things you would like to bring love into on a piece of paper and place it outside during the full moon. As you gaze at the full moon, take a deep breath and visualize yourself becoming more and more loved in these areas. Repeat the following chant three times: "Full moon, bring me love and joy. Fill my heart with happiness and peace."

Full Moon Manifestation Spell

Write down your goals and desires on a piece of paper and place it outside during the full moon. As you gaze at the full moon, take a deep breath and visualize yourself manifesting these things. Repeat the following chant three times: "Full moon, bring my desires to life. Manifest my goals, dreams, and aspirations."

Full Moon Bathing Spell

On the night of a full moon, fill your bathtub with warm water and add several drops of lavender essential oil. Light a white candle and place it near the bathtub. Sit in the bathtub, allowing the full moon's light to shine on you. As you soak, imagine yourself being surrounded by healing light and positive energy. Repeat the following chant three times: "Under the full moon's light, I am healed and made bright. So mote it be." After the bath, wrap yourself in a white towel to symbolize being wrapped in the full moon's light.

Full Moon Abundance Spell

Write down the areas of your life that you would like to bring abundance to on a piece of paper and place it outside during the full moon. As you gaze at the full moon, take a deep breath and visualize yourself becoming more and more abundant in these areas. Repeat the following chant three times: "Full moon, bring me abundance and prosperity. Fill my life with joy, happiness, and success."

Full Moon Confidence Spell

Write down the things you would like to become more confident in on a piece of paper and place it outside during the full moon. As you gaze at the full moon, take a deep breath and visualize yourself becoming more and more confident in these areas. Repeat the following chant three times: "Full moon, bring me confidence and strength. Fill me with courage, power, and determination."

Full Moon Energy Spell

Write down the areas of your life that you would like to bring more energy to on a piece of paper and place it outside during the full moon. As you gaze at the full moon, take a deep breath and visualize yourself becoming more and more energized in these areas. Repeat the following chant three times: "Full moon, bring me energy and vitality. Fill me with life, power, and strength."

Full Moon Mediation Spell

On the night of a full moon, find a quiet place to sit down and meditate. Light a white candle and place it in front of you. Close your eyes and visualize the full moon shining down on you, surrounding you with healing light. Repeat the following chant three times: "Under the full moon's light, I am healed and made bright. So mote it be." Stay in this meditative state for as long as you like, then return to your daily life feeling refreshed and rejuvenated.

Full Moon Anointing Spell

On the night of a full moon, prepare a small bowl of olive oil. Light a white candle and place it near the bowl of oil. Dip your index finger into the oil, then anoint your forehead, heart, and solar plexus, repeating the following chant three times: "Under the full moon's light, I am healed and made bright. So mote it be." After the anointing, blow out the candle and carry the feeling of healing and rejuvenation with you.

Full Moon Protection Spell

Write down the things you would like to be protected from on a piece of paper and place it outside during the full moon. As you gaze at the full moon, take a deep breath and visualize yourself being protected from these things. Repeat the following chant three times: "Full moon, protect me from harm. Surround me with love, light, and peace."

Full Moon Garden Spell

On the night of a full moon, go outside and find a quiet spot in your garden or a nearby park. Sit down, close your eyes, and take a few deep breaths. Visualize yourself surrounded by a circle of white light, which protects and heals you. Repeat the following chant three times: "Under the full moon's light, I am healed and made bright. So mote it be." Stay in this meditative state for as long as you like, then return to your home feeling refreshed and rejuvenated.

Full Moon Oil Spell

On the night of a full moon, prepare a small bottle of olive oil. Anoint the bottle with a white candle, repeating the following chant three times: "Under the full moon's light, this oil is charged and made bright. So mote it be." Use the oil to anoint yourself or someone else who needs healing. The full moon's energy will be infused into the oil, providing healing and rejuvenation.

Waning Moon Spells

Waning Moon spells are those performed during the period of the lunar cycle where the moon is decreasing in size and transitioning from a full moon to a new moon. This phase of the moon is associated with release, letting go, and endings. Waning Moon spells are typically used to remove negative energy, break bad habits, and release negative emotions or thought patterns. Some common materials used in Waning Moon spells include black candles, sage, sea salt, and protective herbs such as rosemary or lavender. When performing Waning Moon spells, it is important to focus on letting go of the things in your life that no longer serve you and to invite in positive change and growth. These spells can be performed alone or with a group, and can be as simple or elaborate as you wish. Whether you write out a list of what you want to release and burn it, or conduct a full-fledged ritual, Waning Moon spells can be a powerful tool for promoting personal growth and spiritual evolution.

Letting Go Spell

For this spell, you will need a piece of paper, a pen, and a candle. Light the candle and sit quietly, focusing on what you need to release from your life. Write down on the piece of paper what it is you need to let go of, and be specific. Fold the paper and hold it in both hands. Close your eyes and visualize yourself releasing the thing you wrote down. Say the following words: "By the power of the waning moon, I release this from my life. So mote it be." Place the paper under the candle and let it burn completely.

Healing Spell

For this spell, you will need a green candle and a piece of rose quartz. Light the green candle and hold the rose quartz in your hand. Close your eyes and visualize yourself surrounded by a warm and comforting light. See yourself being healed of any physical, emotional, or spiritual pain. Say the following words: "By the power of the waning moon, I call forth healing energy. So mote it be." Hold the rose quartz to your heart and keep it with you as a reminder of the healing energy.

Protection Spell

For this spell, you will need a black candle, salt, and a piece of amethyst. Light the black candle and sprinkle salt in a circle around it. Hold the amethyst in your hand and focus on your intention of protection. Say the following words: "By the power of the waning moon, I call forth protection for myself and those I love. So mote it be." Keep the amethyst with you for added protection.

Prosperity Spell

For this spell, you will need a green candle, cinnamon, and a piece of citrine. Light the green candle and sprinkle cinnamon around it. Hold the citrine in your hand and focus on your intention of prosperity. Say the following words: "By the power of the waning moon, I call forth abundance and prosperity. So mote it be." Keep the citrine with you as a symbol of prosperity.

Curses Reversal Spell

For this spell, you will need a white candle, rosemary, and a piece of black tourmaline. Light the white candle and sprinkle rosemary around it. Hold the black tourmaline in your hand and focus on reversing any curses or negative energy that may be affecting you. Say the following words: "By the power of the waning moon, I reverse any curses or negative energy. So mote it be." Keep the black tourmaline with you for added protection against negativity.

Waning Moon Break the Cycle Spell

You will need: a piece of black cord or ribbon, a white candle, and a fireproof container. Light the white candle and hold the black cord or ribbon in your hands. Repeat the following incantation three times: "By the power of the waning moon, I break the cycle of negativity in my life. So mote it be." Tie the cord or ribbon around the candle and place it in the fireproof container. Allow the candle to burn down completely.

Waning Moon Wealth Spell

To perform this spell, you will need a green candle and some money oil. Light the candle and recite the following incantation: "Money come to me, as the moon wanes away, abundance flows my way." Anoint the candle with the money oil and let it burn down completely. Repeat this spell for nine nights in a row for best results.

Waning Moon Protection Spell

For this spell, you will need a white candle and some protective oil. Light the candle and recite the following incantation: "Protection be mine, as the moon wanes, harm stays far behind." Anoint the candle with the protective oil and let it burn down completely. Repeat this spell for nine nights in a row.

Waning Moon Banishing Spell

You will need: a piece of black cloth, a needle and thread, and a white candle. Cut the black cloth into a small square, about the size of your hand. Sew the edges together to form a small pouch. Light the white candle and hold the pouch in your hands. Focus on the things you want to banish from your life. Repeat the following incantation three times: "By the power of the waning moon, I banish these things from my life. So mote it be." Allow the candle to burn down completely, then bury the pouch in the ground.

Goodbye Negativity Spell

For this spell, you will need a black candle and some sage. Light the candle and waft the sage smoke around yourself while reciting the following incantation: "Negativity, be gone, as the moon wanes, my life shines on." Repeat this spell for nine nights in a row.

Waning Moon Recharge Spell

For this spell, you will need a blue candle and some lavender oil. Light the candle and recite the following incantation: "Energy be replenished, as the moon wanes, my strength returns." Anoint the candle with the lavender oil and let it burn down completely. Repeat this spell for nine nights in a row.

Waning Moon Release Spell

For this spell, you will need a red candle and some rose petals. Light the candle and recite the following incantation: "Release and let go, as the moon wanes, I am free to grow." Sprinkle the rose petals around the candle and let it burn down completely. Repeat this spell for nine nights in a row.

Spell Jar Recipes

Spell jars are a powerful and versatile tool for manifestation, protection, and spiritual growth. They are created by filling a jar with a combination of ingredients that correspond to a specific intention. The ingredients can include herbs, crystals, oils, and other materials, depending on the desired outcome. Spell jars can be used for a variety of purposes, from attracting abundance and love, to banishing negative energy and promoting peace and harmony. To make a spell jar, simply gather the necessary ingredients, bless and purify them, and layer them into the jar while focusing on your intention. Seal the jar with a lid or wax, and allow it to sit in a quiet, safe place to infuse with energy and bring your intention to life.

Wealth Spell Jar

Ingredients:

- A glass jar with a tight-fitting lid
- Green stones or crystals such as peridot, malachite, or aventurine
- Rice
- Fresh basil leaves
- Cinnamon sticks
- Coins or small gold-colored objects
- Olive oil

Instructions:

- Cleanse and bless your jar, stones, and ingredients to clear any negative energy.
- Fill the jar halfway with the rice.
- Place the basil leaves on top of the rice.
- Place the green stones or crystals on top of the basil.
- Place the cinnamon sticks and gold-colored objects on top of the stones.
- Fill the jar to the top with the rice.
- Pour the olive oil over the top of the rice until it covers everything.
- Close the lid tightly and shake the jar to mix the ingredients together.
- Charge the jar with your intention for financial abundance by holding it in your hands, visualizing green light filling the jar, and repeating affirmations or incantations for wealth and prosperity.
- Keep the jar in a safe place, preferably near your front door or in your wealth corner.

Love Spell Jar

Ingredients:

- A glass jar with a tight-fitting lid
- Pink stones or crystals such as rose quartz, rhodonite, or stilbite
- Rice
- Fresh rose petals
- Cinnamon sticks
- Small heart-shaped objects
- Sweet almond oil

Instructions:

- Cleanse and bless your jar, stones, and ingredients to clear any negative energy.
- Fill the jar halfway with the rice.
- Place the rose petals on top of the rice.
- Place the pink stones or crystals on top of the petals.
- Place the cinnamon sticks and heart-shaped objects on top of the stones.
- Fill the jar to the top with the rice.
- Pour the sweet almond oil over the top of the rice until it covers everything.
- Close the lid tightly and shake the jar to mix the ingredients together.
- Charge the jar with your intention for love and relationships by holding it in your hands, visualizing pink light filling the jar, and repeating affirmations or incantations for love and romance.
- Keep the jar in a safe place, preferably near your bed or in your love corner.

Protection Spell Jar

Ingredients:

- A glass jar with a tight-fitting lid
- Black stones or crystals such as black tourmaline, obsidian, or onyx
- Salt
- Fresh rosemary sprigs
- Iron nails or pins
- Small protective symbols or talismans
- Frankincense oil

Instructions:

- Cleanse and bless your jar, stones, and ingredients to clear any negative energy.
- Fill the jar halfway with the salt.
- Place the rosemary sprigs on top of the salt.
- Place the black stones or crystals on top of the rosemary.
- Place the iron nails or pins and protective symbols on top of the stones.
- Fill the jar to the top with the salt.
- Pour the frankincense oil over the top of the salt until it covers everything.
- Close the lid tightly and shake the jar to mix the ingredients together.
- Charge the jar with your intention for protection and safety by holding it in your hands, visualizing black light filling the jar

Spell Jar for Abundance and Prosperity

You will need:

- A glass jar with a tight-fitting lid
- Rice
- Allspice
- Cinnamon sticks
- Orange peel

Instructions:

- Fill the jar with a layer of rice, then sprinkle allspice on top.
- Add a layer of cinnamon sticks, followed by a layer of orange peel.
- Close the jar tightly and shake it gently to mix the ingredients.
- Repeat the following incantation while holding the jar in your hands: "Abundance and prosperity, flow into my life. Bring me wealth and good fortune, so mote it be."
- Place the jar in a sunny place, such as a windowsill, for one week.
- After one week, open the jar and sprinkle the contents around your home or office to attract abundance and prosperity.

Spell Jar for Purification and Protection

You will need:

- A glass jar with a tight-fitting lid
- Sea salt
- Sage leaves
- Rose petals
- Black peppercorns

Instructions:

- Fill the jar with a layer of sea salt, then add a layer of sage leaves.
- Sprinkle rose petals on top of the sage leaves, and finish with a layer of black peppercorns.
- Close the jar tightly and shake it gently to mix the ingredients.
- Repeat the following incantation while holding the jar in your hands: "Protection and purification, cleanse and purify my energy. Keep me safe and free from negativity, so mote it be."
- Place the jar in a dark place, such as a closet or cupboard, for one week.
- After one week, open the jar and pour the contents into the earth, or dispose of it in a respectful manner.

Spell Jar for Healing and Renewal

You will need:

- A glass jar with a tight-fitting lid
- Epsom salt
- Rosemary leaves
- Lavender flowers
- Clear quartz crystals

Instructions:

- Fill the jar with a layer of Epsom salt, then sprinkle rosemary leaves on top.
- Add a layer of lavender flowers, followed by a layer of clear quartz crystals.
- Close the jar tightly and shake it gently to mix the ingredients.
- Repeat the following incantation while holding the jar in your hands: "Healing and renewal, restore my body and soul. Renew my energy and bring me peace, so mote it be."
- Place the jar in a quiet place, such as a meditation room or beside your bed, for one week.
- After one week, open the jar and pour the contents into a warm bath to soak and allow the healing and renewal energies to permeate your body.

Money Spell Jar

Ingredients:

- A green glass jar with a tight-fitting lid
- Green stones or crystals such as aventurine, jade, or green calcite
- Salt
- Fresh basil leaves
- Coins
- Cinnamon sticks
- Patchouli oil

Instructions:

- Cleanse and bless your jar, stones, and ingredients to clear any negative energy.
- Fill the jar halfway with the salt. Place the basil leaves on top of the salt.
- Place the green stones or crystals on top of the basil. Place the coins and cinnamon sticks on top of the stones.
- Fill the jar to the top with the salt. Pour the patchouli oil over the top of the salt until it covers everything.
- Close the lid tightly and shake the jar to mix the ingredients together.
- Charge the jar with your intention for financial abundance by holding it in your hands, visualizing green light filling the jar and attracting money to you.
- Keep the jar in a place where you can see it often, such as on your altar or in your office, to reinforce your intention.
- Repeat the following chant three times: "Money flow, to and fro.
- This jar holds power, abundance hour after hour."

www.WitchcraftMagick.com